JAMESTOWN EDUCATION

Reading Fluency

Reader's Record

Level
I

Camille L. Z. Blachowicz, Ph.D.

JAMESTOWN EDUCATION

Reading Fluency

Reader's Record

Level
I

Camille L. Z. Blachowicz, Ph.D.

Mc Graw Hill **Glencoe**

New York, New York   Columbus, Ohio   Chicago, Illinois   Peoria, Illinois   Woodland Hills, California

JAMESTOWN ⚓ EDUCATION

Glencoe

The *McGraw·Hill* Companies

Send all inquiries to:
Glencoe/McGraw-Hill
8787 Orion Place
Columbus, OH 43240-4027

ISBN 0-07-845706-8
Printed in the United States of America.
6 7 8 9 10 021 09 08 07

Contents

The passages in this book are taken from the following sources.

How to Use These Books

The Reading Fluency *Reader* contains 72 reading passages. The accompanying *Reader's Record* contains two copies of each of these passages and includes a place for marking *miscues*. You and your partner will take turns using the *Reader*. Each of you will need your own *Reader's Record*. You will also need a stopwatch or a timer.

What Are Miscues?

Miscues are errors or slips that all readers make. These include the following:
- a mispronounced word
- a word substituted for the correct word
- an inserted word
- a skipped word

Repeating a word or correcting oneself immediately is not counted as a miscue.

What Procedure Do I Follow?

1. Work with a partner. One partner is the reader; the other partner is the recorder.

2. Suppose that you are the first to read aloud. Read a selection from the *Reader* as your partner marks any miscues you make on the corresponding page in your *Reader's Record*. The recorder's job is to listen carefully and make a tick mark above each place in the text where a miscue occurs, and to make a slash mark indicating where you stop reading after "Time!" is called.

3. The recorder says when to start and calls "Time!" after a minute.

4. After the reading, the recorder:
- counts the number of words read, using the number guides at the right-hand side of the passage, and records the Total Words Read
- writes the total number of miscues for each line in the far right-hand column labeled Miscues. Totals and records the miscues on the Total Errors line
- subtracts Total Errors from Total Words Read to find the Correct Words Per Minute (WPM) and records that score on the Correct WPM line

5. You review the *Reader's Record*, noting your miscues. Discuss with your partner the characteristics of good reading you have displayed. Then rate your own performance and mark the scale at the bottom of the page.

6. Change roles with your partner and repeat the procedure.

7. You and your partner then begin a second round of reading the same passage. When it is your turn to read, try to improve in pace, expression, and accuracy over the first reading.

8. After completing two readings, record your Correct WPM scores in the back of your *Reader's Record*. Follow the directions on the graph.

Nonfiction

from **Woman in the Mists:**
The Story of Dian Fossey and the
Mountain Gorillas of Africa
by Farley Mowat

First Reading

	Words Read	Miscues

Today Sanweke and I were charged by two gorillas and it   11   _____

wasn't a bluff charge—they really meant it. We were about one   23   _____

hundred and fifty feet directly downhill from a group when a   34   _____

silverback and a female decided to eradicate us. They gave us a   46   _____

split second of warning with screams and roars that seemed to   57   _____

come from every direction at once before they descended in a   68   _____

gallop that shook the ground. I was determined to stand fast, but   80   _____

when they broke through the foliage at a dead run directly above   92   _____

me, I felt my legs retreating in spite of what I've read about   105   _____

gorillas not charging fully. I paused long enough to try to dissuade   117   _____

them with my voice, which only seemed to aggravate them more,   128   _____

if possible; and when their long, yellow canines and wild eyes   139   _____

were no less than two feet away, I took a very ungainly nosedive   152   _____

into the thick foliage alongside the trail. They whizzed on by,   163   _____

caught up in their own momentum. It's a good thing they didn't   175   _____

come back to attack, for I was certainly in no position to defend   188   _____

myself. It may have taken only a split second to dive into that   201   _____

foliage, but it took about fifteen minutes to extract myself—what   212   _____

a tangle!   214   _____

Needs Work   1   2   3   4   5   **Excellent**
Paid attention to punctuation

Needs Work   1   2   3   4   5   **Excellent**
Sounded good

Total Words Read   _____

Total Errors   − _____

Correct WPM   _____

from **Woman in the Mists:**

The Story of Dian Fossey and the

Mountain Gorillas of Africa

by Farley Mowat

Second Reading

	Words Read	Miscues

Today Sanweke and I were charged by two gorillas and it | 11 | _____

wasn't a bluff charge—they really meant it. We were about one | 23 | _____

hundred and fifty feet directly downhill from a group when a | 34 | _____

silverback and a female decided to eradicate us. They gave us a | 46 | _____

split second of warning with screams and roars that seemed to | 57 | _____

come from every direction at once before they descended in a | 68 | _____

gallop that shook the ground. I was determined to stand fast, but | 80 | _____

when they broke through the foliage at a dead run directly above | 92 | _____

me, I felt my legs retreating in spite of what I've read about | 105 | _____

gorillas not charging fully. I paused long enough to try to dissuade | 117 | _____

them with my voice, which only seemed to aggravate them more, | 128 | _____

if possible; and when their long, yellow canines and wild eyes | 139 | _____

were no less than two feet away, I took a very ungainly nosedive | 152 | _____

into the thick foliage alongside the trail. They whizzed on by, | 163 | _____

caught up in their own momentum. It's a good thing they didn't | 175 | _____

come back to attack, for I was certainly in no position to defend | 188 | _____

myself. It may have taken only a split second to dive into that | 201 | _____

foliage, but it took about fifteen minutes to extract myself—what | 212 | _____

a tangle! | 214 | _____

Needs Work   1 2 3 4 5   Excellent
Paid attention to punctuation

Needs Work   1 2 3 4 5   Excellent
Sounded good

Total Words Read   _____

Total Errors − _____

Correct WPM   _____

from *The Mysterious Island*
by Jules Verne

Fiction

	Words Read	Miscues

A balloon was being swept along by a hurricane at a speed of   13 _____

more than a hundred miles an hour. In the basket swinging below   25 _____

it were five passengers. The air between them and the surface of   37 _____

the water was filled with heavy mist.   44 _____

    Where had that balloon come from? The hurricane had been   54 _____

raging for five days and the balloon could not have traveled less   66 _____

than two thousand miles every twenty-four hours, so it must have   77 _____

come from very far away.   82 _____

    In any case, the passengers had no way of knowing how far   94 _____

they had come. Moving at the same speed as the wind, they did   107 _____

not feel it. The mist around them was so thick that they could not   121 _____

even tell if it was night or day. The balloon had stayed so high   135 _____

that they had not been able to see or hear anything below them.   148 _____

Only now, when they had begun sinking rapidly, did they realize   159 _____

that they were in danger of falling into the ocean.   169 _____

    When they had lightened the balloon by throwing out their   179 _____

weapons, ammunition, food and supplies, it rose to an altitude of   190 _____

forty-five hundred feet.   193 _____

    They spent the night in terrible anxiety. At dawn the storm   204 _____

began to show signs of dying down. By eleven o'clock the mist   216 _____

was gone and the wind was less strong. But the balloon was again   229 _____

sinking.   230 _____

Needs Work   1 2 3 4 5   Excellent
Paid attention to punctuation

Needs Work   1 2 3 4 5   Excellent
Sounded good

Total Words Read _____

Total Errors – _____

Correct WPM _____

2

Fiction

from *The Mysterious Island*
by Jules Verne

	Words Read	Miscues

A balloon was being swept along by a hurricane at a speed of | 13 | _____
more than a hundred miles an hour. In the basket swinging below | 25 | _____
it were five passengers. The air between them and the surface of | 37 | _____
the water was filled with heavy mist. | 44 | _____

Where had that balloon come from? The hurricane had been | 54 | _____
raging for five days and the balloon could not have traveled less | 66 | _____
than two thousand miles every twenty-four hours, so it must have | 77 | _____
come from very far away. | 82 | _____

In any case, the passengers had no way of knowing how far | 94 | _____
they had come. Moving at the same speed as the wind, they did | 107 | _____
not feel it. The mist around them was so thick that they could not | 121 | _____
even tell if it was night or day. The balloon had stayed so high | 135 | _____
that they had not been able to see or hear anything below them. | 148 | _____
Only now, when they had begun sinking rapidly, did they realize | 159 | _____
that they were in danger of falling into the ocean. | 169 | _____

When they had lightened the balloon by throwing out their | 179 | _____
weapons, ammunition, food and supplies, it rose to an altitude of | 190 | _____
forty-five hundred feet. | 193 | _____

They spent the night in terrible anxiety. At dawn the storm | 204 | _____
began to show signs of dying down. By eleven o'clock the mist | 216 | _____
was gone and the wind was less strong. But the balloon was again | 229 | _____
sinking. | 230 | _____

Needs Work 1 2 3 4 5 Excellent
Paid attention to punctuation

Needs Work 1 2 3 4 5 Excellent
Sounded good

Total Words Read _____

Total Errors − _____

Correct WPM _____

3
Fiction

from *Summer of My German Soldier*
by Bette Greene

First Reading

	Words Read	Miscues

Jimmy Wells pointed to the last passenger car. "There!" — 9 — ____

Everyone hurried toward the end of the train in time to see — 21 — ____
two GIs with their side arms still strapped in their holsters step — 33 — ____
quickly from the car. Then came the Germans. The crowd moved — 44 — ____
back slightly, leaving a one-person-wide path between themselves — 52 — ____
and the train. — 55 — ____

The prisoners were unhandcuffed, unchained young men — 62 — ____
carrying regulation Army duffel bags. They wore fresh blue denim — 72 — ____
pants and matching shirts, and if it hadn't been for the black — 84 — ____
"POW" stenciled across their shirt backs you could easily have — 94 — ____
mistaken them for an ordinary crew from the Arkansas Public — 104 — ____
Works Department sent out to repair a stretch of highway. I tried — 116 — ____
to read their faces for brutality, terror, humiliation—something. — 125 — ____
But the only thing I sensed was a kind of relief at finally having — 139 — ____
arrived at their destination. — 143 — ____

"Nazis!" A woman's voice shouted. And this time I knew for — 154 — ____
sure that it was Mrs. Benn. — 160 — ____

A blond prisoner who was stepping off the train at that — 171 — ____
moment stopped short then smiled and waved. It was as though — 182 — ____
he believed, or wanted to believe, that Mrs. Benn's call was — 193 — ____
nothing more than a friendly American greeting. — 200 — ____

I raised my hand, but before I completed a full wave Mary — 212 — ____
Wren pressed it down, shaking her head. — 219 — ____

Needs Work 1 2 3 4 5 Excellent
Paid attention to punctuation

Needs Work 1 2 3 4 5 Excellent
Sounded good

Total Words Read _____

Total Errors − _____

Correct WPM _____

3

Fiction

from *Summer of My German Soldier*
by Bette Greene

	Words Read	Miscues
Jimmy Wells pointed to the last passenger car. "There!"	9	_____
Everyone hurried toward the end of the train in time to see	21	_____
two GIs with their side arms still strapped in their holsters step	33	_____
quickly from the car. Then came the Germans. The crowd moved	44	_____
back slightly, leaving a one-person-wide path between themselves	52	_____
and the train.	55	_____
The prisoners were unhandcuffed, unchained young men	62	_____
carrying regulation Army duffel bags. They wore fresh blue denim	72	_____
pants and matching shirts, and if it hadn't been for the black	84	_____
"POW" stenciled across their shirt backs you could easily have	94	_____
mistaken them for an ordinary crew from the Arkansas Public	104	_____
Works Department sent out to repair a stretch of highway. I tried	116	_____
to read their faces for brutality, terror, humiliation—something.	125	_____
But the only thing I sensed was a kind of relief at finally having	139	_____
arrived at their destination.	143	_____
"Nazis!" A woman's voice shouted. And this time I knew for	154	_____
sure that it was Mrs. Benn.	160	_____
A blond prisoner who was stepping off the train at that	171	_____
moment stopped short then smiled and waved. It was as though	182	_____
he believed, or wanted to believe, that Mrs. Benn's call was	193	_____
nothing more than a friendly American greeting.	200	_____
I raised my hand, but before I completed a full wave Mary	212	_____
Wren pressed it down, shaking her head.	219	_____

Needs Work   1   2   3   4   5   Excellent
Paid attention to punctuation

Needs Work   1   2   3   4   5   Excellent
Sounded good

Total Words Read _____

Total Errors − _____

Correct WPM _____

from *Lift Every Voice*
by Dorothy Sterling and Benjamin Quarles

4 Nonfiction

First Reading

	Words Read	Miscues

Hampton—its full name was Hampton Normal and Agricultural   9   _____
Institute—was one of a group of schools for Negroes established   20   _____
after the Civil War. In addition to book-learning, General Samuel   30   _____
Armstrong, Hampton's founder, taught his pupils the niceties of   39   _____
daily living that they had had no chance to learn under slavery.   51   _____

[Booker T. Washington's] first lesson came on the night of his   62   _____
arrival when he was given a bed to sleep in. Should he crawl   75   _____
under the sheets? Lie on top of them? Only after watching the   87   _____
other boys did he decide to sleep in between. Lesson number two   99   _____
was the toothbrush, lesson number three the tablecloth. For the   109   _____
first time in his sixteen years, the son of the plantation cook sat   122   _____
down at a table to eat, and used a napkin, knife, and fork.   135   _____

Booker spent three happy years at Hampton. Supporting   143   _____
himself by working as the janitor, he learned everything that the   154   _____
school had to offer—geography, grammar, history, science, and   163   _____
practical instruction in farming and handicrafts. A teacher gave   172   _____
him private lessons in public speaking, drilling him until he spoke   183   _____
clearly and emphasized important words in order to hold the   193   _____
interest of his audience. He became a leader in Hampton's   203   _____
debating society and a commencement speaker at his graduation.   212   _____

Needs Work   1   2   3   4   5   Excellent
Paid attention to punctuation

Needs Work   1   2   3   4   5   Excellent
Sounded good

Total Words Read _____

Total Errors − _____

Correct WPM _____

from *Lift Every Voice*

by Dorothy Sterling and Benjamin Quarles

	Words Read	Miscues
Hampton—its full name was Hampton Normal and Agricultural	9	_____
Institute—was one of a group of schools for Negroes established	20	_____
after the Civil War. In addition to book-learning, General Samuel	30	_____
Armstrong, Hampton's founder, taught his pupils the niceties of	39	_____
daily living that they had had no chance to learn under slavery.	51	_____
[Booker T. Washington's] first lesson came on the night of his	62	_____
arrival when he was given a bed to sleep in. Should he crawl	75	_____
under the sheets? Lie on top of them? Only after watching the	87	_____
other boys did he decide to sleep in between. Lesson number two	99	_____
was the toothbrush, lesson number three the tablecloth. For the	109	_____
first time in his sixteen years, the son of the plantation cook sat	122	_____
down at a table to eat, and used a napkin, knife, and fork.	135	_____
Booker spent three happy years at Hampton. Supporting	143	_____
himself by working as the janitor, he learned everything that the	154	_____
school had to offer—geography, grammar, history, science, and	163	_____
practical instruction in farming and handicrafts. A teacher gave	172	_____
him private lessons in public speaking, drilling him until he spoke	183	_____
clearly and emphasized important words in order to hold the	193	_____
interest of his audience. He became a leader in Hampton's	203	_____
debating society and a commencement speaker at his graduation.	212	_____

Needs Work   1   2   3   4   5   Excellent
Paid attention to punctuation

Needs Work   1   2   3   4   5   Excellent
Sounded good

Total Words Read _____

Total Errors − _____

Correct WPM _____

5 *Nonfiction*

from *Trial by Ice*
by K. M. Kostyal

	Words Read	Miscues

Shackleton had hoped that a vast plain of snow and ice lay | 12 | _____

between him and [the South Pole]. But he was wrong. The high, | 24 | _____

jagged Transantarctic Mountains stood in his path. But luck was | 34 | _____

on his side. In early December he and his men came upon one of | 48 | _____

the few passes through the mountains. A glacier they called the | 59 | _____

Golden Gateway led them to a stupendous ice field 30 miles wide | 71 | _____

and more than 100 miles long. [One of the men] believed that it | 84 | _____

"must be the largest in the world. . . ." Though deep snow, | 94 | _____

crevasses, and other obstacles marred its glistening blue surface, | 103 | _____

still it beckoned like a wide road, and Shackleton and his men | 115 | _____

took it. | 117 | _____

A week later they were still climbing the glacier, scrambling | 127 | _____

over high ridges of ice, roped together to keep from falling into | 139 | _____

hidden crevasses. As they climbed higher, the cold and wind grew | 150 | _____

worse, and frostbite threatened their fingers, toes, and faces. They | 160 | _____

were running low on food and had little fuel left either to cook | 173 | _____

with or to melt snow for drinking water. Yet they kept going, and | 186 | _____

by December 28 they at last left the glacier behind and became | 198 | _____

the first humans ever to set foot on the smooth, vast ice cap that | 212 | _____

covers the South Pole. | 216 | _____

Needs Work 1 2 3 4 5 Excellent
Paid attention to punctuation

Needs Work 1 2 3 4 5 Excellent
Sounded good

Total Words Read _____

Total Errors − _____

Correct WPM _____

from *Trial by Ice*
by K. M. Kostyal

	Words Read	Miscues
Shackleton had hoped that a vast plain of snow and ice lay	12	_____
between him and [the South Pole]. But he was wrong. The high,	24	_____
jagged Transantarctic Mountains stood in his path. But luck was	34	_____
on his side. In early December he and his men came upon one of	48	_____
the few passes through the mountains. A glacier they called the	59	_____
Golden Gateway led them to a stupendous ice field 30 miles wide	71	_____
and more than 100 miles long. [One of the men] believed that it	84	_____
"must be the largest in the world. . . ." Though deep snow,	94	_____
crevasses, and other obstacles marred its glistening blue surface,	103	_____
still it beckoned like a wide road, and Shackleton and his men	115	_____
took it.	117	_____
A week later they were still climbing the glacier, scrambling	127	_____
over high ridges of ice, roped together to keep from falling into	139	_____
hidden crevasses. As they climbed higher, the cold and wind grew	150	_____
worse, and frostbite threatened their fingers, toes, and faces. They	160	_____
were running low on food and had little fuel left either to cook	173	_____
with or to melt snow for drinking water. Yet they kept going, and	186	_____
by December 28 they at last left the glacier behind and became	198	_____
the first humans ever to set foot on the smooth, vast ice cap that	212	_____
covers the South Pole.	216	_____

Needs Work   1   2   3   4   5   Excellent
Paid attention to punctuation

Needs Work   1   2   3   4   5   Excellent
Sounded good

Total Words Read _____

Total Errors – _____

Correct WPM _____

6 Thirteen Days in October

Nonfiction

First Reading

	Words Read	Miscues

John F. Kennedy, President of the United States, peered at the — 11 —

photographs taken by a U-2 spy plane flying high over Cuba. — 22 —

Nikita Khrushchev, premier of the Soviet Union, was installing — 31 —

offensive nuclear weapons just 90 miles off the Florida coast. — 41 —

It was October 15, 1962. — 46 —

    Kennedy called his advisers together. Some favored an — 54 —

immediate air strike and an invasion of Cuba; some thought the — 65 —

United States should put up a naval blockade around Cuba to — 76 —

turn away Soviet ships carrying weapons. Finally Kennedy — 84 —

decided. The navy would put up a blockade. — 92 —

    Then on October 26, Kennedy received a letter from — 101 —

Khrushchev proposing that the Soviets would remove the missiles — 110 —

in exchange for a U.S. pledge never to invade Cuba. Before — 121 —

Kennedy could reply, a second Khrushchev letter arrived proposing — 130 —

a different solution. Khrushchev wanted U.S. missiles in Turkey — 139 —

removed in exchange for the removal of the Cuban missiles. — 149 —

    The terms of Khrushchev's first letter were acceptable, but not — 159 —

the terms of the second. So Kennedy ignored the second letter. He — 171 —

answered the first letter instead. He replied on October 27th, and — 182 —

the next day a message came from Khrushchev. Yes, the Soviet — 193 —

Union would accept the terms as stated in the President's letter. — 204 —

Somehow during those 13 days in October 1962, a war was — 215 —

avoided. — 216 —

Needs Work   1 2 3 4 5   Excellent
Paid attention to punctuation

Needs Work   1 2 3 4 5   Excellent
Sounded good

Total Words Read _____

Total Errors − _____

Correct WPM _____

Thirteen Days in October

Second Reading

	Words Read	Miscues

John F. Kennedy, President of the United States, peered at the | 11 | _____
photographs taken by a U-2 spy plane flying high over Cuba. | 22 | _____
Nikita Khrushchev, premier of the Soviet Union, was installing | 31 | _____
offensive nuclear weapons just 90 miles off the Florida coast. | 41 | _____
It was October 15, 1962. | 46 | _____

Kennedy called his advisers together. Some favored an | 54 | _____
immediate air strike and an invasion of Cuba; some thought the | 65 | _____
United States should put up a naval blockade around Cuba to | 76 | _____
turn away Soviet ships carrying weapons. Finally Kennedy | 84 | _____
decided. The navy would put up a blockade. | 92 | _____

Then on October 26, Kennedy received a letter from | 101 | _____
Khrushchev proposing that the Soviets would remove the missiles | 110 | _____
in exchange for a U.S. pledge never to invade Cuba. Before | 121 | _____
Kennedy could reply, a second Khrushchev letter arrived proposing | 130 | _____
a different solution. Khrushchev wanted U.S. missiles in Turkey | 139 | _____
removed in exchange for the removal of the Cuban missiles. | 149 | _____

The terms of Khrushchev's first letter were acceptable, but not | 159 | _____
the terms of the second. So Kennedy ignored the second letter. He | 171 | _____
answered the first letter instead. He replied on October 27th, and | 182 | _____
the next day a message came from Khrushchev. Yes, the Soviet | 193 | _____
Union would accept the terms as stated in the President's letter. | 204 | _____
Somehow during those 13 days in October 1962, a war was | 215 | _____
avoided. | 216 | _____

Needs Work 1 2 3 4 5 Excellent	**Total Words Read** _____
Paid attention to punctuation	
Needs Work 1 2 3 4 5 Excellent	**Total Errors** − _____
Sounded good	**Correct WPM** _____

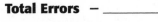

7

Fiction

from *Norby and the Oldest Dragon*
by Janet and Isaac Asimov

∾

	Words Read	Miscues
Cadet Jefferson Wells was having a difficult time packing his	10	_____
suitcase because his room at Space Academy was crowded with	20	_____
three other cadets bubbling with curiosity and questions about	29	_____
Jeff's secret destination.	32	_____
Norby was no help, either. Although he didn't ask questions	42	_____
because he knew where they were going, he was trying to impress	54	_____
the other cadets with the fact that he was an efficient personal	66	_____
robot in spite of being small, barrel-shaped, and having only	76	_____
half a head. Waving his extensible arms, Norby gave advice.	86	_____
Lots of advice.	89	_____
"Jeff, don't put your spare boots on the bottom because	99	_____
everything on top will get lumpy. Put them into the spaces left	111	_____
when you've finished everything else. And don't forget to pack	121	_____
your new toothpastebrush because the one in the suitcase is	131	_____
empty. And I recommend at least two extra pairs of socks because	143	_____
the last time we went anywhere you didn't even have one to	155	_____
change into . . ."	157	_____
As Norby droned on and the other cadets laughed, Jeff	167	_____
rebelliously put in only one extra pair of socks. After all, they	179	_____
were only going for the weekend.	185	_____
Although he was an orphaned fifteen-year-old, Jeff had	193	_____
managed to survive many dubious adventures, most of them caused	203	_____
by the fact that his so-called teaching robot contained weird alien	214	_____
parts and mixed everything up at unexpected moments.	222	_____

Needs Work   1   2   3   4   5   Excellent
Paid attention to punctuation

Needs Work   1   2   3   4   5   Excellent
Sounded good

Total Words Read _____

Total Errors − _____

Correct WPM _____

from *Norby and the Oldest Dragon*

by Janet and Isaac Asimov

	Words Read	Miscues

Cadet Jefferson Wells was having a difficult time packing his — 10

suitcase because his room at Space Academy was crowded with — 20

three other cadets bubbling with curiosity and questions about — 29

Jeff's secret destination. — 32

Norby was no help, either. Although he didn't ask questions — 42

because he knew where they were going, he was trying to impress — 54

the other cadets with the fact that he was an efficient personal — 66

robot in spite of being small, barrel-shaped, and having only — 76

half a head. Waving his extensible arms, Norby gave advice. — 86

Lots of advice. — 89

"Jeff, don't put your spare boots on the bottom because — 99

everything on top will get lumpy. Put them into the spaces left — 111

when you've finished everything else. And don't forget to pack — 121

your new toothpastebrush because the one in the suitcase is — 131

empty. And I recommend at least two extra pairs of socks because — 143

the last time we went anywhere you didn't even have one to — 155

change into . . ." — 157

As Norby droned on and the other cadets laughed, Jeff — 167

rebelliously put in only one extra pair of socks. After all, they — 179

were only going for the weekend. — 185

Although he was an orphaned fifteen-year-old, Jeff had — 193

managed to survive many dubious adventures, most of them caused — 203

by the fact that his so-called teaching robot contained weird alien — 214

parts and mixed everything up at unexpected moments. — 222

Needs Work 1 2 3 4 5 **Excellent**
Paid attention to punctuation

Needs Work 1 2 3 4 5 **Excellent**
Sounded good

Total Words Read _____

Total Errors − _____

Correct WPM _____

8
Fiction

from *The Great Interactive Dream Machine*

by Richard Peck

First Reading

	Words Read	Miscues

✠

	Words Read	Miscues
Something had scared [the dog] under the furniture, and I	10	_____
thought I knew what.	14	_____
I followed the smell of a small electrical fire down a long hall	27	_____
to [my best friend] Aaron's room.	33	_____
I pushed open his door. He's got a bed in there and a stack of	48	_____
Byte magazines from the school media center, and a book called	59	_____
Navigating the Internet. But the rest of the room is an ultra-high-	71	_____
tech, state-of-the-art, stand-alone microsystem workstation.	75	_____
It's built around a pair of Big Blue's power PC's with a couple	88	_____
of high-definition TV screens and more add-ons and video assets	98	_____
than you can believe. We're talking mainframe here. It goes to the	110	_____
ceiling, with wires and cables snaking around the floor. Aaron	120	_____
calls it his personalized blendo-technopolis. He uses terms like	129	_____
this, and I don't know what they mean.	137	_____
As late as last winter if Aaron wanted to [experiment with] his	149	_____
data on two keyboards at once, he had to use the computers in	162	_____
the school media center. We were both *this close* to getting in big	175	_____
trouble for being in there when we weren't supposed to be. Now I	188	_____
noticed that his home workstation had doubled in size.	197	_____

Needs Work 1 2 3 4 5 Excellent
Paid attention to punctuation

Needs Work 1 2 3 4 5 Excellent
Sounded good

Total Words Read _____

Total Errors − _____

Correct WPM _____

from *The Great Interactive Dream Machine*

by Richard Peck

	Words Read	Miscues
Something had scared [the dog] under the furniture, and I	10	_____
thought I knew what.	14	_____
I followed the smell of a small electrical fire down a long hall	27	_____
to [my best friend] Aaron's room.	33	_____
I pushed open his door. He's got a bed in there and a stack of	48	_____
Byte magazines from the school media center, and a book called	59	_____
Navigating the Internet. But the rest of the room is an ultra-high-	71	_____
tech, state-of-the-art, stand-alone microsystem workstation.	75	_____
It's built around a pair of Big Blue's power PC's with a couple	88	_____
of high-definition TV screens and more add-ons and video assets	98	_____
than you can believe. We're talking mainframe here. It goes to the	110	_____
ceiling, with wires and cables snaking around the floor. Aaron	120	_____
calls it his personalized blendo-technopolis. He uses terms like	129	_____
this, and I don't know what they mean.	137	_____
As late as last winter if Aaron wanted to [experiment with] his	149	_____
data on two keyboards at once, he had to use the computers in	162	_____
the school media center. We were both *this close* to getting in big	175	_____
trouble for being in there when we weren't supposed to be. Now I	188	_____
noticed that his home workstation had doubled in size.	197	_____

Needs Work   1 2 3 4 5   Excellent
Paid attention to punctuation

Needs Work   1 2 3 4 5   Excellent
Sounded good

Total Words Read   _____

Total Errors − _____

Correct WPM   _____

9
Fiction

from *An Ocean Apart, a World Away*
by Lensey Namioka

First Reading

	Words Read	Miscues

One Saturday, the [Pettigrew family] invited me to go with | 10 | _____
them to a football game between Cornell and Yale. I was | 21 | _____
astounded by the loud yells of the spectators. It sounded like a | 33 | _____
revolution breaking out, except that what I had seen of the | 44 | _____
revolution in China had not been quite so noisy. | 53 | _____

Nor could I make any sense of the game, since all I could see | 67 | _____
was a big muddle, with the players crashing into one another. | 78 | _____
Having possession of the ball was apparently very important, but | 88 | _____
I never did catch a glimpse of it. At least I could tell which players | 103 | _____
were on our side and which were against us: The Cornell boys | 115 | _____
wore red, and the Yale boys wore blue. | 123 | _____

Suddenly there was a huge roar, and all the spectators around | 134 | _____
me jumped to their feet. From the yells, I gathered that someone | 146 | _____
had downed a touch—or maybe touched a down. Whatever it | 157 | _____
was, it was obviously a good thing. | 164 | _____

After the roaring died down, somebody blew a whistle, and | 174 | _____
the players left the field. A file of musicians playing various | 185 | _____
instruments marched across the field, reminding me of an old- | 195 | _____
fashioned Chinese funeral. | 197 | _____

"It's halftime," said Mr. Pettigrew. When I didn't understand, | 206 | _____
he explained. "It's like an intermission. Boy, I can use a rest from | 219 | _____
all this excitement." | 222 | _____

Needs Work   1   2   3   4   5   Excellent
Paid attention to punctuation

Needs Work   1   2   3   4   5   Excellent
Sounded good

Total Words Read   _____

Total Errors   − _____

Correct WPM   _____

17

from *An Ocean Apart, a World Away*

by Lensey Namioka

	Words Read	Miscues

One Saturday, the [Pettigrew family] invited me to go with   10   _____
them to a football game between Cornell and Yale. I was   21   _____
astounded by the loud yells of the spectators. It sounded like a   33   _____
revolution breaking out, except that what I had seen of the   44   _____
revolution in China had not been quite so noisy.   53   _____

Nor could I make any sense of the game, since all I could see   67   _____
was a big muddle, with the players crashing into one another.   78   _____
Having possession of the ball was apparently very important, but   88   _____
I never did catch a glimpse of it. At least I could tell which players   103   _____
were on our side and which were against us: The Cornell boys   115   _____
wore red, and the Yale boys wore blue.   123   _____

Suddenly there was a huge roar, and all the spectators around   134   _____
me jumped to their feet. From the yells, I gathered that someone   146   _____
had downed a touch—or maybe touched a down. Whatever it   157   _____
was, it was obviously a good thing.   164   _____

After the roaring died down, somebody blew a whistle, and   174   _____
the players left the field. A file of musicians playing various   185   _____
instruments marched across the field, reminding me of an old-   195   _____
fashioned Chinese funeral.   197   _____

"It's halftime," said Mr. Pettigrew. When I didn't understand,   206   _____
he explained. "It's like an intermission. Boy, I can use a rest from   219   _____
all this excitement."   222   _____

Needs Work   1   2   3   4   5   Excellent
Paid attention to punctuation

Needs Work   1   2   3   4   5   Excellent
Sounded good

Total Words Read   _____

Total Errors   − _____

Correct WPM   _____

10 *Fiction*

from *Dracula*
by Bram Stoker

	Words Read	Miscues

"You know this place, Jonathan. You have copied maps of it, — 11 _____

and you know it at least more than we do. Which is the way to — 26 _____

the chapel?" I had an idea of its direction, though on my former — 39 _____

visit I had not been able to get admission to it; so I led the way, — 55 _____

and after a few wrong turnings found myself opposite a low, — 66 _____

arched oaken door, ribbed with iron bands. "This is the spot," said — 78 _____

the Professor as he turned his lamp on a small map of the house, — 92 _____

copied from the file of my original correspondence regarding the — 102 _____

purchase. With a little trouble we found the key on the bunch — 114 _____

and opened the door. We were prepared for some unpleasantness, — 124 _____

for as we were opening the door a faint, malodorous air seemed — 136 _____

to exhale through the gaps, but none of us ever expected such an — 149 _____

odor as we encountered. None of the others had met the Count — 161 _____

at all at close quarters, and when I had seen him he was either in — 176 _____

the fasting stage of his existence in his rooms or, when he was — 189 _____

gloated with fresh blood, in a ruined building open to the air; but — 202 _____

here the place was small and close, and the long disuse had made — 215 _____

the air stagnant and foul. — 220 _____

Needs Work   1   2   3   4   5   Excellent
Paid attention to punctuation

Needs Work   1   2   3   4   5   Excellent
Sounded good

Total Words Read _____

Total Errors − _____

Correct WPM _____

from *Dracula*

by Bram Stoker

	Words Read	Miscues
"You know this place, Jonathan. You have copied maps of it,	11	_____
and you know it at least more than we do. Which is the way to	26	_____
the chapel?" I had an idea of its direction, though on my former	39	_____
visit I had not been able to get admission to it; so I led the way,	55	_____
and after a few wrong turnings found myself opposite a low,	66	_____
arched oaken door, ribbed with iron bands. "This is the spot," said	78	_____
the Professor as he turned his lamp on a small map of the house,	92	_____
copied from the file of my original correspondence regarding the	102	_____
purchase. With a little trouble we found the key on the bunch	114	_____
and opened the door. We were prepared for some unpleasantness,	124	_____
for as we were opening the door a faint, malodorous air seemed	136	_____
to exhale through the gaps, but none of us ever expected such an	149	_____
odor as we encountered. None of the others had met the Count	161	_____
at all at close quarters, and when I had seen him he was either in	176	_____
the fasting stage of his existence in his rooms or, when he was	189	_____
gloated with fresh blood, in a ruined building open to the air; but	202	_____
here the place was small and close, and the long disuse had made	215	_____
the air stagnant and foul.	220	_____

Needs Work   1   2   3   4   5   Excellent
_____
            Paid attention to punctuation

Needs Work   1   2   3   4   5   Excellent
_____
                Sounded good

Total Words Read _____

Total Errors − _____

Correct WPM _____

11
Fiction

from *The Hound of the Baskervilles*
by Arthur Conan Doyle

First Reading

	Words Read	Miscues

✽

	Words Read	Miscues
Mr. Sherlock Holmes, who was usually very late in the	10	_____
mornings, save upon those not infrequent occasions when he was	20	_____
up all night, was seated at the breakfast table. I stood upon the	33	_____
hearth-rug and picked up the stick which our visitor had left	44	_____
behind him the night before. It was a fine, thick piece of wood,	57	_____
bulbous-headed, of the sort which is known as a "Penang lawyer."	68	_____
Just under the head was a broad silver band, nearly an inch	80	_____
across. "To James Mortimer, M.R.C.S., from his friends of the	90	_____
C.C.H.," was engraved upon it, with the date "1884." It was just	102	_____
such a stick as the old-fashioned family practitioner used to	112	_____
carry—dignified, solid, and reassuring.	117	_____
"Well, Watson, what do you make of it?"	125	_____
Holmes was sitting with his back to me, and I had given him	138	_____
no sign of my occupation.	143	_____
"How did you know what I was doing? I believe you have eyes	156	_____
in the back of your head."	162	_____
"I have, at least, a well-polished silver plated coffee-pot in	172	_____
front of me," said he. "But, tell me, Watson, what do you make of	186	_____
our visitor's stick? Since we have been so unfortunate as to miss	198	_____
him and have no notion of his errand, this accidental souvenir	209	_____
becomes of importance. Let me hear you reconstruct the man by	220	_____
an examination of it."	224	_____

Needs Work   1 2 3 4 5   Excellent
Paid attention to punctuation

Needs Work   1 2 3 4 5   Excellent
Sounded good

Total Words Read _____

Total Errors − _____

Correct WPM _____

11

Fiction

from *The Hound of the Baskervilles*
by Arthur Conan Doyle

	Words Read	Miscues

Mr. Sherlock Holmes, who was usually very late in the | 10 | _____

mornings, save upon those not infrequent occasions when he was | 20 | _____

up all night, was seated at the breakfast table. I stood upon the | 33 | _____

hearth-rug and picked up the stick which our visitor had left | 44 | _____

behind him the night before. It was a fine, thick piece of wood, | 57 | _____

bulbous-headed, of the sort which is known as a "Penang lawyer." | 68 | _____

Just under the head was a broad silver band, nearly an inch | 80 | _____

across. "To James Mortimer, M.R.C.S., from his friends of the | 90 | _____

C.C.H.," was engraved upon it, with the date "1884." It was just | 102 | _____

such a stick as the old-fashioned family practitioner used to | 112 | _____

carry—dignified, solid, and reassuring. | 117 | _____

"Well, Watson, what do you make of it?" | 125 | _____

Holmes was sitting with his back to me, and I had given him | 138 | _____

no sign of my occupation. | 143 | _____

"How did you know what I was doing? I believe you have eyes | 156 | _____

in the back of your head." | 162 | _____

"I have, at least, a well-polished silver plated coffee-pot in | 172 | _____

front of me," said he. "But, tell me, Watson, what do you make of | 186 | _____

our visitor's stick? Since we have been so unfortunate as to miss | 198 | _____

him and have no notion of his errand, this accidental souvenir | 209 | _____

becomes of importance. Let me hear you reconstruct the man by | 220 | _____

an examination of it." | 224 | _____

Needs Work   1   2   3   4   5   Excellent
Paid attention to punctuation

Needs Work   1   2   3   4   5   Excellent
Sounded good

Total Words Read _____

Total Errors − _____

Correct WPM _____

12 *Nonfiction*

from *The Buried City of Pompeii*
by Shelley Tanaka

First Reading

	Words Read	Miscues

~~~~

Vesuvius erupted on August 24, A.D. 79. [The city of] Pompeii had been experiencing earth tremors for a few days, and many people still remembered an earthquake that had damaged much of the city seventeen years before. But they did not realize that they were living in the lap of a deadly volcano.

At about 1 P.M., the mountain roared, and her summit cracked open. A huge column of pumice and ash shot up into the air like a rocket. When the column reached the height of 12 miles, it spread out like a fountain. Ash and pumice began to fall to the ground.

In horror, the people of Pompeii had to decide whether to flee or stay. Most chose to run, and soon the gates were clogged with humans and pack animals trying to push their way out of the city. Others hid in their homes, hoping that by some miracle, the rain of fire would soon stop.

But it didn't. With every passing hour, another 6 inches of pumice covered Pompeii. By late afternoon, the sky was almost black. Roofs caved in. Walls collapsed as earth tremors rocked the city.

At midnight, the column of ash and pumice finally collapsed back to earth. That's when superhot rock and gas spewed up out of the volcano and began to flow down the mountain, smothering and burning up the countryside.

Words Read
11
22
31
43
53
64
78
90
102
104
116
129
142
154
159
170
180
190
192
202
214
225
230

Needs Work   1   2   3   4   5   Excellent
Paid attention to punctuation

Needs Work   1   2   3   4   5   Excellent
Sounded good

Total Words Read _____

Total Errors − _____

Correct WPM _____

from *The Buried City of Pompeii*
by Shelley Tanaka

	Words Read	Miscues

Vesuvius erupted on August 24, A.D. 79. [The city of] Pompeii | 11 | _____ |
had been experiencing earth tremors for a few days, and many | 22 | _____ |
people still remembered an earthquake that had damaged much | 31 | _____ |
of the city seventeen years before. But they did not realize that | 43 | _____ |
they were living in the lap of a deadly volcano. | 53 | _____ |

At about 1 P.M., the mountain roared, and her summit cracked | 64 | _____ |
open. A huge column of pumice and ash shot up into the air like | 78 | _____ |
a rocket. When the column reached the height of 12 miles, it | 90 | _____ |
spread out like a fountain. Ash and pumice began to fall to | 102 | _____ |
the ground. | 104 | _____ |

In horror, the people of Pompeii had to decide whether to flee | 116 | _____ |
or stay. Most chose to run, and soon the gates were clogged with | 129 | _____ |
humans and pack animals trying to push their way out of the city. | 142 | _____ |
Others hid in their homes, hoping that by some miracle, the rain | 154 | _____ |
of fire would soon stop. | 159 | _____ |

But it didn't. With every passing hour, another 6 inches of | 170 | _____ |
pumice covered Pompeii. By late afternoon, the sky was almost | 180 | _____ |
black. Roofs caved in. Walls collapsed as earth tremors rocked | 190 | _____ |
the city. | 192 | _____ |

At midnight, the column of ash and pumice finally collapsed | 202 | _____ |
back to earth. That's when superhot rock and gas spewed up out | 214 | _____ |
of the volcano and began to flow down the mountain, smothering | 225 | _____ |
and burning up the countryside. | 230 | _____ |

Needs Work   1   2   3   4   5   Excellent
Paid attention to punctuation

Needs Work   1   2   3   4   5   Excellent
Sounded good

Total Words Read _____

Total Errors − _____

Correct WPM _____

13

Nonfiction

from *Turn of the Century*
by Nancy Smiler Levinson

	Words Read	Miscues

❨❩❪

One night in July 1881, fifteen-year-old Kate Shelley and her | 10 | _____
mother stood anxiously looking through a window of their Iowa | 20 | _____
farmhouse. Outside a raging storm was swelling the waters of | 30 | _____
Honey Creek, which emptied into the swiftly flowing Des Moines | 40 | _____
River. | 41 | _____

They had already rescued the livestock from the flooded barn | 51 | _____
and moved the animals to higher ground, and they had calmed | 62 | _____
the frightened younger children in their beds. But the storm grew | 73 | _____
worse, and their worries heightened. | 78 | _____

Nearby lay the tracks of the Chicago and Northwestern | 87 | _____
Railroad, where Kate's father, an Irish immigrant, had worked as a | 98 | _____
section foreman before he died in an accident on the job. About | 110 | _____
eleven o'clock, Kate and her mother heard an engine whistle. But | 121 | _____
no train was scheduled in either direction at that hour. Suddenly, | 132 | _____
they heard a crash and the hissing of steam. They knew at once | 145 | _____
what had happened. | 148 | _____

The No. 11, an engine from the Moingona station, had been | 159 | _____
sent ahead to check the track's safety for an express passenger | 170 | _____
train scheduled to pass through at midnight. The Honey Creek | 180 | _____
wooden bridge had been washed out, and the No. 11 had | 191 | _____
plunged into the river below. | 196 | _____

The women were horrified. Kate knew she had to help the men | 208 | _____
and get word to the station operator to stop the midnight train. | 220 | _____

Needs Work   1   2   3   4   5   Excellent
Paid attention to punctuation

Needs Work   1   2   3   4   5   Excellent
Sounded good

Total Words Read _____

Total Errors − _____

Correct WPM _____

from *Turn of the Century*

by Nancy Smiler Levinson

	Words Read	Miscues

➦➦➦

One night in July 1881, fifteen-year-old Kate Shelley and her   10 _____
mother stood anxiously looking through a window of their Iowa   20 _____
farmhouse. Outside a raging storm was swelling the waters of   30 _____
Honey Creek, which emptied into the swiftly flowing Des Moines   40 _____
River.   41 _____

They had already rescued the livestock from the flooded barn   51 _____
and moved the animals to higher ground, and they had calmed   62 _____
the frightened younger children in their beds. But the storm grew   73 _____
worse, and their worries heightened.   78 _____

Nearby lay the tracks of the Chicago and Northwestern   87 _____
Railroad, where Kate's father, an Irish immigrant, had worked as a   98 _____
section foreman before he died in an accident on the job. About   110 _____
eleven o'clock, Kate and her mother heard an engine whistle. But   121 _____
no train was scheduled in either direction at that hour. Suddenly,   132 _____
they heard a crash and the hissing of steam. They knew at once   145 _____
what had happened.   148 _____

The No. 11, an engine from the Moingona station, had been   159 _____
sent ahead to check the track's safety for an express passenger   170 _____
train scheduled to pass through at midnight. The Honey Creek   180 _____
wooden bridge had been washed out, and the No. 11 had   191 _____
plunged into the river below.   196 _____

The women were horrified. Kate knew she had to help the men   208 _____
and get word to the station operator to stop the midnight train.   220 _____

Needs Work   1   2   3   4   5   Excellent
Paid attention to punctuation

Needs Work   1   2   3   4   5   Excellent
Sounded good

Total Words Read _____

Total Errors − _____

Correct WPM _____

14
Nonfiction

from *Keepers and Creatures*
at the National Zoo
by Peggy Thomson

First Reading

	Words Read	Miscues

First thing, keeper Morna Holden has her heart in her mouth   11   _____
as she greets and good-mornings everyone on her line in the   22   _____
Elephant House—the two Asian elephants, the rhino, and   31   _____
especially African elephant Nancy, who was sick yesterday.   39   _____

Today Nancy is herself again—clear-eyed and alert. Morna   48   _____
expected her to be. All the same, she's relieved. She tells Nancy as   61   _____
much while she hoists herself into the enclosure to run a hand   73   _____
over Nancy's waving trunk and her fanning ears and to hug a   85   _____
foreleg. In the fond, grumbling way of an elephant keeper to an   97   _____
elephant, she complains about an animal's pigging out on junk   107   _____
food, for that's what she suspects Nancy did.   115   _____

Yesterday Morna found the elephant flopped out flat, and the   125   _____
first times she'd gotten Nancy up and standing, all four and a half   138   _____
tons of her, Nancy'd sunk to her knees and flopped again.   149   _____
Indigestion, by the look of it, an elephant-sized bellyache, which   159   _____
doesn't happen often but happens. Nancy has a way of reaching   170   _____
out her trunk over the rail and accepting all-wrong gifts from the   182   _____
public. She'd been at it on Saturday. In the past she's taken   194   _____
candies, wrappers, mittens, cartons. Not hamburgers—she rejects   202   _____
them. Once, according to her keepers, she downed a backpack,   212   _____
though elephant keepers have been known to exaggerate.   220   _____

Needs Work   1   2   3   4   5   Excellent
Paid attention to punctuation

Needs Work   1   2   3   4   5   Excellent
Sounded good

Total Words Read   _____

Total Errors   − _____

Correct WPM   _____

from *Keepers and Creatures at the National Zoo*

by Peggy Thomson

Second Reading

	Words Read	Miscues

First thing, keeper Morna Holden has her heart in her mouth | 11 | _____
as she greets and good-mornings everyone on her line in the | 22 | _____
Elephant House—the two Asian elephants, the rhino, and | 31 | _____
especially African elephant Nancy, who was sick yesterday. | 39 | _____

Today Nancy is herself again—clear-eyed and alert. Morna | 48 | _____
expected her to be. All the same, she's relieved. She tells Nancy as | 61 | _____
much while she hoists herself into the enclosure to run a hand | 73 | _____
over Nancy's waving trunk and her fanning ears and to hug a | 85 | _____
foreleg. In the fond, grumbling way of an elephant keeper to an | 97 | _____
elephant, she complains about an animal's pigging out on junk | 107 | _____
food, for that's what she suspects Nancy did. | 115 | _____

Yesterday Morna found the elephant flopped out flat, and the | 125 | _____
first times she'd gotten Nancy up and standing, all four and a half | 138 | _____
tons of her, Nancy'd sunk to her knees and flopped again. | 149 | _____
Indigestion, by the look of it, an elephant-sized bellyache, which | 159 | _____
doesn't happen often but happens. Nancy has a way of reaching | 170 | _____
out her trunk over the rail and accepting all-wrong gifts from the | 182 | _____
public. She'd been at it on Saturday. In the past she's taken | 194 | _____
candies, wrappers, mittens, cartons. Not hamburgers—she rejects | 202 | _____
them. Once, according to her keepers, she downed a backpack, | 212 | _____
though elephant keepers have been known to exaggerate. | 220 | _____

Needs Work   1 2 3 4 5   Excellent
Paid attention to punctuation

Needs Work   1 2 3 4 5   Excellent
Sounded good

Total Words Read _____

Total Errors − _____

Correct WPM _____

from *Mountain Light*

by Laurence Yep

Fiction

	Words Read	Miscues

I recognized the Stranger, Yammer. One moment he was running | 10 | _____

with his fists pumping at the air, and the next moment he was | 23 | _____

flying through the air and sprawling in the dirt. | 32 | _____

He scrambled to his feet almost immediately, and we could see | 43 | _____

that his face was so contorted by fear that it no longer seemed | 56 | _____

quite human. His lips were twisted back to reveal his teeth, and | 68 | _____

his eyelids were drawn up so that his eyes were whiter and wider | 81 | _____

than a normal human's. He took one step and fell with a grunt. | 94 | _____

He rolled over onto his back as he raised one leg and clasped | 107 | _____

his ankle. He squinted in pain as if he had twisted it on some | 121 | _____

unseen root. And suddenly the torchlight was bright beneath us | 131 | _____

as the other villagers surrounded the Stranger. | 138 | _____

His eyes opened in terror and he gave a start—as if he saw us | 153 | _____

hiding in the branches of the tree, but the villagers were too | 165 | _____

occupied with him to turn around and notice us. I thought for a | 178 | _____

moment that he might try to save himself by turning us in as spies | 192 | _____

or something; but he kept silent, though the villagers narrowed | 202 | _____

the ring around him. | 206 | _____

Needs Work   1 2 3 4 5   Excellent
Paid attention to punctuation

Needs Work   1 2 3 4 5   Excellent
Sounded good

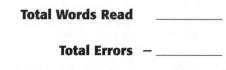

Total Words Read   _____

Total Errors   − _____

Correct WPM   _____

15

Fiction

from *Mountain Light*

by Laurence Yep

	Words Read	Miscues

I recognized the Stranger, Yammer. One moment he was running | 10 | _____
with his fists pumping at the air, and the next moment he was | 23 | _____
flying through the air and sprawling in the dirt. | 32 | _____

He scrambled to his feet almost immediately, and we could see | 43 | _____
that his face was so contorted by fear that it no longer seemed | 56 | _____
quite human. His lips were twisted back to reveal his teeth, and | 68 | _____
his eyelids were drawn up so that his eyes were whiter and wider | 81 | _____
than a normal human's. He took one step and fell with a grunt. | 94 | _____

He rolled over onto his back as he raised one leg and clasped | 107 | _____
his ankle. He squinted in pain as if he had twisted it on some | 121 | _____
unseen root. And suddenly the torchlight was bright beneath us | 131 | _____
as the other villagers surrounded the Stranger. | 138 | _____

His eyes opened in terror and he gave a start—as if he saw us | 153 | _____
hiding in the branches of the tree, but the villagers were too | 165 | _____
occupied with him to turn around and notice us. I thought for a | 178 | _____
moment that he might try to save himself by turning us in as spies | 192 | _____
or something; but he kept silent, though the villagers narrowed | 202 | _____
the ring around him. | 206 | _____

Needs Work   1 2 3 4 5   Excellent
Paid attention to punctuation

Needs Work   1 2 3 4 5   Excellent
Sounded good

Total Words Read _____

Total Errors − _____

Correct WPM _____

from *On the Bus with Joanna Cole:*
A Creative Autobiography
by Joanna Cole, with Wendy Saul

Nonfiction

First Reading

	Words Read	Miscues

My father was a very intelligent man who could do just about   12 _____
anything, but he didn't think of himself as intelligent. That's   22 _____
because he had dyslexia and never could read very well as a child.   35 _____
In those days, people didn't know about dyslexia, and his teachers   46 _____
punished and shamed him for it. Later in life he taught himself to   59 _____
read the newspaper, but he never became a real reader.   69 _____

One day, when I was about twelve or thirteen, I was lying on   82 _____
the sofa immersed in a novel. My father came by and asked with   95 _____
genuine curiosity, "What is it like to read a book like that?" I told   109 _____
him about the experience of reading—about how the words on   120 _____
the page seem to disappear and you become lost in the story,   132 _____
seeing pictures and hearing voices in your head. I felt a new   144 _____
appreciation of an intense pleasure that I had simply taken for   155 _____
granted before and sorry that my father could not share it.   166 _____

You might think that a man who did not read or write very   179 _____
much could not be a strong influence on a writer. But that isn't   192 _____
true at all of my father and me. He was a fabulous storyteller.   205 _____

Needs Work   1 2 3 4 5   Excellent
Paid attention to punctuation

Needs Work   1 2 3 4 5   Excellent
Sounded good

Total Words Read _____

Total Errors − _____

Correct WPM _____

from *On the Bus with Joanna Cole:*
A Creative Autobiography
by Joanna Cole, with Wendy Saul

Second Reading

	Words Read	Miscues

My father was a very intelligent man who could do just about 〔12〕
anything, but he didn't think of himself as intelligent. That's 〔22〕
because he had dyslexia and never could read very well as a child. 〔35〕
In those days, people didn't know about dyslexia, and his teachers 〔46〕
punished and shamed him for it. Later in life he taught himself to 〔59〕
read the newspaper, but he never became a real reader. 〔69〕

One day, when I was about twelve or thirteen, I was lying on 〔82〕
the sofa immersed in a novel. My father came by and asked with 〔95〕
genuine curiosity, "What is it like to read a book like that?" I told 〔109〕
him about the experience of reading—about how the words on 〔120〕
the page seem to disappear and you become lost in the story, 〔132〕
seeing pictures and hearing voices in your head. I felt a new 〔144〕
appreciation of an intense pleasure that I had simply taken for 〔155〕
granted before and sorry that my father could not share it. 〔166〕

You might think that a man who did not read or write very 〔179〕
much could not be a strong influence on a writer. But that isn't 〔192〕
true at all of my father and me. He was a fabulous storyteller. 〔205〕

Needs Work   1   2   3   4   5   Excellent
Paid attention to punctuation

Needs Work   1   2   3   4   5   Excellent
Sounded good

Total Words Read _____

Total Errors − _____

Correct WPM _____

17

Nonfiction

from *Eleanor Roosevelt:*
A Life of Discovery
by Russell Freedman

First Reading

	Words Read	Miscues

Never before had the American people seen a First Lady like
Eleanor Roosevelt. Soon she was flying off all over the country,
serving as her husband's personal investigative reporter and
gathering material for her columns, articles, radio talks, and
books. Reporters who covered the White House and traveled
with Mrs. Roosevelt marveled at her energy and pace.

She was a frequent flier at a time when a trip in an airplane
was considered a great adventure. Once, in order to impress the
public with the ease and safety of air travel, Amelia Earhart
invited the First Lady to join her on a flight from Washington to
Baltimore. They both wore evening dresses. "How do you feel
being piloted by a woman?" Eleanor was asked. "Absolutely safe,"
she replied. "I'd give a lot to do it myself!"

Eleanor seemed to go everywhere. Since she could travel more
freely than Franklin, she again became his "eyes and ears." She
dropped in on coal miners in Appalachia, slum-dwellers in Puerto
Rico, and sharecroppers in their tarpaper shacks in southern
cotton fields. And she inspected government relief projects from
one end of the country to the other, "often managing to arrive
without advance notice so that they could not be polished up for
my inspection."

Words Read
11
22
30
39
48
57
71
82
93
106
116
126
136
146
157
167
176
185
197
209
211

Needs Work   1   2   3   4   5   Excellent
Paid attention to punctuation

Needs Work   1   2   3   4   5   Excellent
Sounded good

Total Words Read _____

Total Errors – _____

Correct WPM _____

17

Nonfiction

from *Eleanor Roosevelt:*
A Life of Discovery
by Russell Freedman

	Words Read	Miscues

Never before had the American people seen a First Lady like 11 _____
Eleanor Roosevelt. Soon she was flying off all over the country, 22 _____
serving as her husband's personal investigative reporter and 30 _____
gathering material for her columns, articles, radio talks, and 39 _____
books. Reporters who covered the White House and traveled 48 _____
with Mrs. Roosevelt marveled at her energy and pace. 57 _____

She was a frequent flier at a time when a trip in an airplane 71 _____
was considered a great adventure. Once, in order to impress the 82 _____
public with the ease and safety of air travel, Amelia Earhart 93 _____
invited the First Lady to join her on a flight from Washington to 106 _____
Baltimore. They both wore evening dresses. "How do you feel 116 _____
being piloted by a woman?" Eleanor was asked. "Absolutely safe," 126 _____
she replied. "I'd give a lot to do it myself!" 136 _____

Eleanor seemed to go everywhere. Since she could travel more 146 _____
freely than Franklin, she again became his "eyes and ears." She 157 _____
dropped in on coal miners in Appalachia, slum-dwellers in Puerto 167 _____
Rico, and sharecroppers in their tarpaper shacks in southern 176 _____
cotton fields. And she inspected government relief projects from 185 _____
one end of the country to the other, "often managing to arrive 197 _____
without advance notice so that they could not be polished up for 209 _____
my inspection." 211 _____

Needs Work   1 2 3 4 5   Excellent
   Paid attention to punctuation

Needs Work   1 2 3 4 5   Excellent
   Sounded good

Total Words Read   _____

Total Errors − _____

Correct WPM   _____

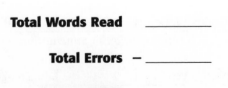

18

Nonfiction

from *Behind Barbed Wire:*

The Imprisonment of Japanese Americans During World War II

by Daniel S. Davis

First Reading

	Words Read	Miscues

Early in January 1942, the Justice Department caved in to   10 _____

military pressure and agreed to stricter controls on enemy aliens.   20 _____

This included spot raids on their homes.   27 _____

Soon, FBI agents raided homes of Japanese residents. They   36 _____

peppered them with questions about their loyalty and searched   45 _____

for forbidden items.   48 _____

The raids sparked a new wave of fear in the Japanese   59 _____

community. People who had kept mementos of the old country   69 _____

now followed the lead of those who had destroyed them just after   81 _____

Pearl Harbor. Many . . . wives [of Japanese citizens living in the   91 _____

U.S.] packed traveling bags for their husbands, so that if the FBI   103 _____

took them away in the dead of night, they would have a fresh   116 _____

change of clothes and toilet articles with them.   124 _____

Hundreds of FBI agents trundled out of Japanese   132 _____

neighborhoods loaded down with cartons of contraband—items   140 _____

enemy aliens were forbidden to have in their possession. These   150 _____

included cameras; knives, including Boy Scout hunting knives; and   159 _____

explosives sometimes used by farmers. The results of these raids   169 _____

could easily have been predicted. Attorney General Biddle   177 _____

reported to the president: 181 _____

"We have not uncovered through these searches any   189 _____

dangerous persons that we could not otherwise know about."   198 _____

Needs Work   1   2   3   4   5   Excellent
Paid attention to punctuation

Needs Work   1   2   3   4   5   Excellent
Sounded good

Total Words Read _____

Total Errors − _____

Correct WPM _____

from *Behind Barbed Wire:*
The Imprisonment of Japanese Americans
During World War II
by Daniel S. Davis

Second Reading

	Words Read	Miscues
Early in January 1942, the Justice Department caved in to	10	_____
military pressure and agreed to stricter controls on enemy aliens.	20	_____
This included spot raids on their homes.	27	_____
Soon, FBI agents raided homes of Japanese residents. They	36	_____
peppered them with questions about their loyalty and searched	45	_____
for forbidden items.	48	_____
The raids sparked a new wave of fear in the Japanese	59	_____
community. People who had kept mementos of the old country	69	_____
now followed the lead of those who had destroyed them just after	81	_____
Pearl Harbor. Many . . . wives [of Japanese citizens living in the	91	_____
U.S.] packed traveling bags for their husbands, so that if the FBI	103	_____
took them away in the dead of night, they would have a fresh	116	_____
change of clothes and toilet articles with them.	124	_____
Hundreds of FBI agents trundled out of Japanese	132	_____
neighborhoods loaded down with cartons of contraband—items	140	_____
enemy aliens were forbidden to have in their possession. These	150	_____
included cameras; knives, including Boy Scout hunting knives; and	159	_____
explosives sometimes used by farmers. The results of these raids	169	_____
could easily have been predicted. Attorney General Biddle	177	_____
reported to the president:	181	_____
"We have not uncovered through these searches any	189	_____
dangerous persons that we could not otherwise know about."	198	_____

Needs Work   1   2   3   4   5   Excellent
        Paid attention to punctuation

Needs Work   1   2   3   4   5   Excellent
        Sounded good

Total Words Read _____

Total Errors − _____

Correct WPM _____

19
Fiction

from "A White Heron"
by Sarah Orne Jewett

	Words Read	Miscues

Sylvia felt her way easily. She had often climbed there, and knew | 12 | _____
that higher still one of the oak's upper branches chafed against the | 24 | _____
pine trunk, just where its lower boughs were set close together. | 35 | _____
There, when she made the dangerous pass from one tree to the | 47 | _____
other, the great enterprise would really begin. | 54 | _____

 She crept out along the swaying oak limb at last, and took the | 67 | _____
daring step across into the old pine tree. The way was harder than | 80 | _____
she thought; she must reach far and hold fast. The sharp dry twigs | 93 | _____
caught and held her and scratched her like angry talons, the pitch | 105 | _____
made her thin little fingers clumsy and stiff as she went round | 117 | _____
and round the tree's great stem, higher and higher upward. The | 128 | _____
sparrows and robins in the woods below were beginning to wake | 139 | _____
and twitter to the dawn, yet it seemed much lighter there aloft in | 152 | _____
the pine tree, and the child knew she must hurry if her project | 165 | _____
were to be of any use. | 171 | _____

 The tree seemed to lengthen itself out as she went up, and to | 184 | _____
reach farther and farther upward. It was like a great mainmast to | 196 | _____
the voyaging earth. | 199 | _____

Needs Work   1   2   3   4   5   Excellent
Paid attention to punctuation

Needs Work   1   2   3   4   5   Excellent
Sounded good

Total Words Read   _____

Total Errors   − _____

Correct WPM   _____

from "A White Heron"
by Sarah Orne Jewett

	Words Read	Miscues

Sylvia felt her way easily. She had often climbed there, and knew — 12 ——

that higher still one of the oak's upper branches chafed against the — 24 ——

pine trunk, just where its lower boughs were set close together. — 35 ——

There, when she made the dangerous pass from one tree to the — 47 ——

other, the great enterprise would really begin. — 54 ——

She crept out along the swaying oak limb at last, and took the — 67 ——

daring step across into the old pine tree. The way was harder than — 80 ——

she thought; she must reach far and hold fast. The sharp dry twigs — 93 ——

caught and held her and scratched her like angry talons, the pitch — 105 ——

made her thin little fingers clumsy and stiff as she went round — 117 ——

and round the tree's great stem, higher and higher upward. The — 128 ——

sparrows and robins in the woods below were beginning to wake — 139 ——

and twitter to the dawn, yet it seemed much lighter there aloft in — 152 ——

the pine tree, and the child knew she must hurry if her project — 165 ——

were to be of any use. — 171 ——

The tree seemed to lengthen itself out as she went up, and to — 184 ——

reach farther and farther upward. It was like a great mainmast to — 196 ——

the voyaging earth. — 199 ——

Needs Work   1   2   3   4   5   Excellent
Paid attention to punctuation

Needs Work   1   2   3   4   5   Excellent
Sounded good

Total Words Read _____

Total Errors − _____

Correct WPM _____

20 from *So Big*
by Edna Ferber

Fiction

	Words Read	Miscues
The historic old Haymarket on west Randolph Street had become	10	_____
the stand for market gardeners for miles around Chicago. Here	20	_____
they stationed their wagons in preparation for the next day's	30	_____
selling. The wagons stood, close packed, in triple rows, down both	41	_____
sides of the curb and in the middle of the street. The early comer	55	_____
got the advantageous stand. There was no regular allotment of	65	_____
space. Pervus tried to reach the Haymarket by nine at night. Often	77	_____
bad roads made a detour necessary and he was late. That usually	89	_____
meant bad business next day. The men, for the most part, slept on	102	_____
their wagons, curled up on the wagon-seat or stretched out on the	114	_____
sacks. Their horses were stabled and fed in nearby sheds, with	125	_____
more actual comfort than the men themselves. One could get a	136	_____
room for twenty-five cents in one of the ramshackle rooming	146	_____
houses that faced the street. But the rooms were small, stuffy,	157	_____
none too clean; the beds little more comfortable than the wagons.	168	_____
Besides, twenty-five cents! You got twenty-five cents for half a	178	_____
barrel of tomatoes. You got twenty-five cents for a sack of	189	_____
potatoes. Onions brought seventy-five cents a sack. Cabbages	197	_____
went a hundred heads for two dollars, and they were five-pound	208	_____
heads. . . . No; one did not pay out twenty-five cents for the mere	220	_____
privilege of sleeping in a bed.	226	_____

Needs Work   1 2 3 4 5   Excellent
Paid attention to punctuation

Needs Work   1 2 3 4 5   Excellent
Sounded good

Total Words Read _____

Total Errors − _____

Correct WPM _____

from *So Big*
by Edna Ferber

Text	Words Read	Miscues
The historic old Haymarket on west Randolph Street had become	10	_____
the stand for market gardeners for miles around Chicago. Here	20	_____
they stationed their wagons in preparation for the next day's	30	_____
selling. The wagons stood, close packed, in triple rows, down both	41	_____
sides of the curb and in the middle of the street. The early comer	55	_____
got the advantageous stand. There was no regular allotment of	65	_____
space. Pervus tried to reach the Haymarket by nine at night. Often	77	_____
bad roads made a detour necessary and he was late. That usually	89	_____
meant bad business next day. The men, for the most part, slept on	102	_____
their wagons, curled up on the wagon-seat or stretched out on the	114	_____
sacks. Their horses were stabled and fed in nearby sheds, with	125	_____
more actual comfort than the men themselves. One could get a	136	_____
room for twenty-five cents in one of the ramshackle rooming	146	_____
houses that faced the street. But the rooms were small, stuffy,	157	_____
none too clean; the beds little more comfortable than the wagons.	168	_____
Besides, twenty-five cents! You got twenty-five cents for half a	178	_____
barrel of tomatoes. You got twenty-five cents for a sack of	189	_____
potatoes. Onions brought seventy-five cents a sack. Cabbages	197	_____
went a hundred heads for two dollars, and they were five-pound	208	_____
heads. . . . No; one did not pay out twenty-five cents for the mere	220	_____
privilege of sleeping in a bed.	226	_____

Needs Work   1   2   3   4   5   Excellent
Paid attention to punctuation

Needs Work   1   2   3   4   5   Excellent
Sounded good

Total Words Read _____

Total Errors   − _____

Correct WPM _____

21

Nonfiction

from *A Long Hard Journey:*
The Story of the Pullman Porter
by Patricia and Fredrick McKissack

First Reading

	Words Read	Miscues

〜〜〜

	Words Read	Miscues
Once the passengers were comfortably seated [on the train]	9	_____
and their bags were stored, the porter attended to special	19	_____
requests. He might be handing out newspapers, helping a mother	29	_____
with restless children, or pointing out geographic points of	38	_____
interest to first-time travelers or foreign visitors.	45	_____
The Pullman porter's primary focus was the customer's welfare.	54	_____
He was instructed—and very often tested—to answer all calls	65	_____
promptly and courteously, no matter what time the calls were	75	_____
made.	76	_____
When it was time to make the beds, the porter was expected	88	_____
to move with speed and agility. The company rule book was	99	_____
precise. According to Nathaniel Hall, a porter, the rule book	109	_____
specified "the proper handling of the linen closet—the proper	119	_____
method of folding and putting away clean linen and blankets, the	130	_____
correct way of stacking laundry bags and dirty, discarded bedding.	140	_____
A sheet, towel, or pillowcase once unfolded cannot be used again,	151	_____
although it may be spotless. Technically, it is dirty and must make	163	_____
a round trip to the laundry before it can reenter the service."	175	_____
Porters were not allowed to make noise. "Noise was tabooed,"	185	_____
reported Hall. "And even a soft knock on the top of the berth	198	_____
[was] forbidden. A porter must gently shake the curtains on the	209	_____
bedding from without."	212	_____

Needs Work 1 2 3 4 5 Excellent
Paid attention to punctuation

Needs Work 1 2 3 4 5 Excellent
Sounded good

Total Words Read _____

Total Errors − _____

Correct WPM _____

from *A Long Hard Journey:*
The Story of the Pullman Porter
by Patricia and Fredrick McKissack

	Words Read	Miscues

Once the passengers were comfortably seated [on the train] and their bags were stored, the porter attended to special requests. He might be handing out newspapers, helping a mother with restless children, or pointing out geographic points of interest to first-time travelers or foreign visitors.

The Pullman porter's primary focus was the customer's welfare. He was instructed—and very often tested—to answer all calls promptly and courteously, no matter what time the calls were made.

When it was time to make the beds, the porter was expected to move with speed and agility. The company rule book was precise. According to Nathaniel Hall, a porter, the rule book specified "the proper handling of the linen closet—the proper method of folding and putting away clean linen and blankets, the correct way of stacking laundry bags and dirty, discarded bedding. A sheet, towel, or pillowcase once unfolded cannot be used again, although it may be spotless. Technically, it is dirty and must make a round trip to the laundry before it can reenter the service."

Porters were not allowed to make noise. "Noise was tabooed," reported Hall. "And even a soft knock on the top of the berth [was] forbidden. A porter must gently shake the curtains on the bedding from without."

Words Read
9
19
29
38
45
54
65
75
76
88
99
109
119
130
140
151
163
175
185
198
209
212

Needs Work 1 2 3 4 5 Excellent
Paid attention to punctuation

Needs Work 1 2 3 4 5 Excellent
Sounded good

Total Words Read _____

Total Errors − _____

Correct WPM _____

22 Nonfiction

from *Sally Ride:*
America's First Woman in Space
by Carolyn Blacknall

First Reading

	Words Read	Miscues

With the excitement of launch behind them, the STS-7 crew · 10 · _____

settled down to a busy day. Every 90 minutes, *Challenger* · 20 · _____

completed an orbit of the earth. On the seventh orbit, the crew · 32 · _____

planned to launch the Anik-C satellite. · 38 · _____

Anik-C was a Canadian communications satellite. It would · 46 · _____

relay voice, pictures, and information services throughout Canada. · 54 · _____

In the Inuit Indian language, *Anik* means *brother.* · 62 · _____

As the seventh orbit drew near, the astronauts prepared to · 72 · _____

launch the satellite. Bob Crippen and Rick Hauck opened the · 82 · _____

orbiter's payload bay doors and slowly turned the shuttle to the · 93 · _____

correct position. Sally Ride and John Fabian could see into the · 104 · _____

60-foot-long cargo bay through the two small windows in the · 114 · _____

back of the flight deck. Three satellites and two satellite boosters · 125 · _____

were stored there. · 128 · _____

The boosters were needed to push Anik-C and the other · 138 · _____

communications satellite, Palapa-B, into a higher orbit. · 145 · _____

Challenger's orbit was 160 miles above the earth. Both satellites · 155 · _____

had to fly at an altitude of 22,300 miles to stay above the same · 169 · _____

position on the earth. · 173 · _____

Sally and John, floating weightless in the flight deck, started · 183 · _____

the booster rocket spinning. The commander and pilot checked · 192 · _____

Challenger's movement with scientists and computers in Houston. · 200 · _____

When the shuttle was in position, Sally and John launched the · 211 · _____

satellite out of the shuttle's payload bay. · 218 · _____

Needs Work   1   2   3   4   5   Excellent
Paid attention to punctuation

Needs Work   1   2   3   4   5   Excellent
Sounded good

Total Words Read   _____

Total Errors − _____

Correct WPM   _____

22

Nonfiction

from *Sally Ride:*
America's First Woman in Space
by Carolyn Blacknall

	Words Read	Miscues

With the excitement of launch behind them, the STS-7 crew   10 _____

settled down to a busy day. Every 90 minutes, *Challenger*   20 _____

completed an orbit of the earth. On the seventh orbit, the crew   32 _____

planned to launch the Anik-C satellite.   38 _____

Anik-C was a Canadian communications satellite. It would   46 _____

relay voice, pictures, and information services throughout Canada.   54 _____

In the Inuit Indian language, *Anik* means *brother.*   62 _____

As the seventh orbit drew near, the astronauts prepared to   72 _____

launch the satellite. Bob Crippen and Rick Hauck opened the   82 _____

orbiter's payload bay doors and slowly turned the shuttle to the   93 _____

correct position. Sally Ride and John Fabian could see into the   104 _____

60-foot-long cargo bay through the two small windows in the   114 _____

back of the flight deck. Three satellites and two satellite boosters   125 _____

were stored there.   128 _____

The boosters were needed to push Anik-C and the other   138 _____

communications satellite, Palapa-B, into a higher orbit.   145 _____

Challenger's orbit was 160 miles above the earth. Both satellites   155 _____

had to fly at an altitude of 22,300 miles to stay above the same   169 _____

position on the earth.   173 _____

Sally and John, floating weightless in the flight deck, started   183 _____

the booster rocket spinning. The commander and pilot checked   192 _____

Challenger's movement with scientists and computers in Houston.   200 _____

When the shuttle was in position, Sally and John launched the   211 _____

satellite out of the shuttle's payload bay.   218 _____

Needs Work   1 2 3 4 5   Excellent
  Paid attention to punctuation

Needs Work   1 2 3 4 5   Excellent
  Sounded good

Total Words Read _____

Total Errors − _____

Correct WPM _____

23 from "The Speckled Band"
by Arthur Conan Doyle

Fiction

First Reading

	Words Read	Miscues

⍠

I had no keener pleasure than in following Holmes in his   11 _____

professional investigations, and in admiring the rapid deductions, 19 _____

as swift as intuitions, and yet always founded on a logical basis, 31 _____

with which he unraveled the problems which were submitted to   41 _____

him. I rapidly threw on my coat, and was ready in a few minutes   55 _____

to accompany my friend down to the sitting room. A lady dressed   67 _____

in black and heavily veiled, who had been sitting in the window,   79 _____

rose as we entered.   83 _____

"Good morning, madam," said Holmes cheerily. "My name   91 _____

is Sherlock Holmes. This is my friend and associate, Dr. Watson,   102 _____

before whom you can speak as freely as before myself. Ha, I am   115 _____

glad to see that Mrs. Hudson has had the good sense to light the   129 _____

fire. Pray draw up to it, and I shall order you a cup of hot coffee, 145 _____

for I observe that you are shivering."   152 _____

"It is not cold which makes me shiver," said the woman in a   165 _____

low voice, changing her seat as requested.   172 _____

"What then?"   174 _____

"It is fear, Mr. Holmes. It is terror." She raised her veil as she 188 _____

spoke, and we could see that she was indeed in a pitiable state of 202 _____

agitation, her face all drawn and gray, with restless, frightened 212 _____

eyes, like those of some hunted animal.   219 _____

Needs Work   1 2 3 4 5   Excellent
Paid attention to punctuation

Needs Work   1 2 3 4 5   Excellent
Sounded good

Total Words Read _____

Total Errors − _____

Correct WPM _____

23
Fiction

from "The Speckled Band"
by Arthur Conan Doyle

Second Reading

	Words Read	Miscues

I had no keener pleasure than in following Holmes in his — 11

professional investigations, and in admiring the rapid deductions, — 19

as swift as intuitions, and yet always founded on a logical basis, — 31

with which he unraveled the problems which were submitted to — 41

him. I rapidly threw on my coat, and was ready in a few minutes — 55

to accompany my friend down to the sitting room. A lady dressed — 67

in black and heavily veiled, who had been sitting in the window, — 79

rose as we entered. — 83

"Good morning, madam," said Holmes cheerily. "My name — 91

is Sherlock Holmes. This is my friend and associate, Dr. Watson, — 102

before whom you can speak as freely as before myself. Ha, I am — 115

glad to see that Mrs. Hudson has had the good sense to light the — 129

fire. Pray draw up to it, and I shall order you a cup of hot coffee, — 145

for I observe that you are shivering." — 152

"It is not cold which makes me shiver," said the woman in a — 165

low voice, changing her seat as requested. — 172

"What then?" — 174

"It is fear, Mr. Holmes. It is terror." She raised her veil as she — 188

spoke, and we could see that she was indeed in a pitiable state of — 202

agitation, her face all drawn and gray, with restless, frightened — 212

eyes, like those of some hunted animal. — 219

Needs Work 1 2 3 4 5 **Excellent**
Paid attention to punctuation

Needs Work 1 2 3 4 5 **Excellent**
Sounded good

Total Words Read _____

Total Errors − _____

Correct WPM _____

24 from "Appetizer"

by Robert H. Abel

Fiction

	Words Read	Miscues

I lay on the seat panting, curled like a child, shuddered when | 12 | _____

the bear slammed against the pickup's side. The bear pressed her | 23 | _____

nose to the window, then curiously, unceremoniously licked the | 32 | _____

glass with her tongue. I know (and you know) she could have | 44 | _____

shattered the glass with a single blow, and I tried to imagine what | 57 | _____

I should do if indeed she resorted to this simple expedient. | 68 | _____

Fisherman that I am, I had nothing in the cab of the truck to | 82 | _____

defend myself with except a tire iron, and that not readily | 93 | _____

accessible behind the seat I was cowering on. My best defense, | 104 | _____

obviously, was to start the pickup and drive away. | 113 | _____

Just as I sat up to the steering wheel and inserted the key, | 126 | _____

however, Ms. Bear slammed her big paws onto the hood and | 137 | _____

hoisted herself aboard. The pickup shuddered with the weight of | 147 | _____

her, and suddenly the windshield was full of her golden fur. I | 159 | _____

beeped the horn loud and long numerous times, but this had | 170 | _____

about the same effect as my singing, only caused her to shake her | 183 | _____

huge head, which vibrated the truck terribly. She stomped around | 193 | _____

on the hood and then lay down, back against the windshield, | 204 | _____

which now appeared to have been covered by a huge shag rug. | 216 | _____

Needs Work   1 2 3 4 5   Excellent
Paid attention to punctuation

Needs Work   1 2 3 4 5   Excellent
Sounded good

Total Words Read _____

Total Errors − _____

Correct WPM _____

from **"Appetizer"**
by Robert H. Abel

	Words Read	Miscues

I lay on the seat panting, curled like a child, shuddered when | 12 | _____
the bear slammed against the pickup's side. The bear pressed her | 23 | _____
nose to the window, then curiously, unceremoniously licked the | 32 | _____
glass with her tongue. I know (and you know) she could have | 44 | _____
shattered the glass with a single blow, and I tried to imagine what | 57 | _____
I should do if indeed she resorted to this simple expedient. | 68 | _____
Fisherman that I am, I had nothing in the cab of the truck to | 82 | _____
defend myself with except a tire iron, and that not readily | 93 | _____
accessible behind the seat I was cowering on. My best defense, | 104 | _____
obviously, was to start the pickup and drive away. | 113 | _____

Just as I sat up to the steering wheel and inserted the key, | 126 | _____
however, Ms. Bear slammed her big paws onto the hood and | 137 | _____
hoisted herself aboard. The pickup shuddered with the weight of | 147 | _____
her, and suddenly the windshield was full of her golden fur. I | 159 | _____
beeped the horn loud and long numerous times, but this had | 170 | _____
about the same effect as my singing, only caused her to shake her | 183 | _____
huge head, which vibrated the truck terribly. She stomped around | 193 | _____
on the hood and then lay down, back against the windshield, | 204 | _____
which now appeared to have been covered by a huge shag rug. | 216 | _____

Needs Work   1   2   3   4   5   Excellent
Paid attention to punctuation

Needs Work   1   2   3   4   5   Excellent
Sounded good

Total Words Read   _____

Total Errors   − _____

Correct WPM   _____

25

Fiction

from "My Mother and Father"
by Budge Wilson

First Reading

	Words Read	Miscues

I was born in Grace Maternity Hospital in Halifax, entering   10 _____
the world noisily and with confidence, to greet a mother who was   22 _____
already a widow. Far from her home in the south of France, she   35 _____
spent eight solitary days in the hospital, and then wrapped me in   47 _____
a blue blanket and took me home to an empty house.   58 _____

It was early November when we entered that house, and   68 _____
France must have seemed a hundred light-years away. My mother   78 _____
had come to Nova Scotia as a young war bride in 1919, and after   92 _____
ten childless years had finally given birth to her first and last baby. 105 _____
The next several months of my life in that home must have been   118 _____
terrible indeed for her. She and my father had moved from   129 _____
Wolfville to Halifax shortly before he died, and she was therefore   140 _____
living in a strange city as well as in a foreign land. Although she 154 _____
had an almost perfect mastery of English, she retained a slight   165 _____
French accent, and was considered strange, alien, too exotic for   175 _____
safety. As a result, she had few acquaintances, no close friends,   186 _____
and of course no husband. Furthermore, it would be six months   197 _____
before one could expect any semblance of summer to soften   207 _____
Canada's stern, uncompromising East Coast.   212 _____

Needs Work   1 2 3 4 5   Excellent
Paid attention to punctuation

Needs Work   1 2 3 4 5   Excellent
Sounded good

Total Words Read _____

Total Errors − _____

Correct WPM _____

25

Fiction

from "My Mother and Father"

by Budge Wilson

	Words Read	Miscues

I was born in Grace Maternity Hospital in Halifax, entering — 10

the world noisily and with confidence, to greet a mother who was — 22

already a widow. Far from her home in the south of France, she — 35

spent eight solitary days in the hospital, and then wrapped me in — 47

a blue blanket and took me home to an empty house. — 58

It was early November when we entered that house, and — 68

France must have seemed a hundred light-years away. My mother — 78

had come to Nova Scotia as a young war bride in 1919, and after — 92

ten childless years had finally given birth to her first and last baby. — 105

The next several months of my life in that home must have been — 118

terrible indeed for her. She and my father had moved from — 129

Wolfville to Halifax shortly before he died, and she was therefore — 140

living in a strange city as well as in a foreign land. Although she — 154

had an almost perfect mastery of English, she retained a slight — 165

French accent, and was considered strange, alien, too exotic for — 175

safety. As a result, she had few acquaintances, no close friends, — 186

and of course no husband. Furthermore, it would be six months — 197

before one could expect any semblance of summer to soften — 207

Canada's stern, uncompromising East Coast. — 212

Needs Work 1 2 3 4 5 Excellent
Paid attention to punctuation

Needs Work 1 2 3 4 5 Excellent
Sounded good

Total Words Read _____

Total Errors − _____

Correct WPM _____

26

Fiction

from *Matilda*
by Roald Dahl

	Words Read	Miscues

There was a muddy pond at the bottom of Lavender's garden — 11 — _____

and this was the home of a colony of newts. The newt, although — 24 — _____

fairly common in English ponds, is not often seen by ordinary — 35 — _____

people because it is a shy and murky creature. It is an incredibly — 48 — _____

ugly gruesome-looking animal, rather like a baby crocodile but — 57 — _____

with a shorter head. It is quite harmless but doesn't look it. It is — 71 — _____

about six inches long and very slimy, with a greenish-grey skin on — 83 — _____

top and an orange-colored belly underneath. It is, in fact, an — 94 — _____

amphibian, which can live in or out of water. — 103 — _____

That evening Lavender went to the bottom of the garden — 113 — _____

determined to catch a newt. They are swiftly-moving animals and — 123 — _____

not easy to get hold of. She lay on the bank for a long time — 138 — _____

waiting patiently until she spotted a whopper. Then, using her — 148 — _____

school hat as a net, she swooped and caught it. She had lined her — 162 — _____

pencil-box with pond-weed ready to receive the creature, but she — 172 — _____

discovered that it was not easy to get the newt out of the hat and — 187 — _____

into the pencil-box. It wriggled and squirmed like quicksilver and, — 197 — _____

apart from that, the box was only just long enough to take it. — 210 — _____

Needs Work   1   2   3   4   5   Excellent
Paid attention to punctuation

Needs Work   1   2   3   4   5   Excellent
Sounded good

Total Words Read _____

Total Errors − _____

Correct WPM _____

26

Fiction

from *Matilda*

by Roald Dahl

	Words Read	Miscues

There was a muddy pond at the bottom of Lavender's garden ... 11 _____

and this was the home of a colony of newts. The newt, although ... 24 _____

fairly common in English ponds, is not often seen by ordinary ... 35 _____

people because it is a shy and murky creature. It is an incredibly ... 48 _____

ugly gruesome-looking animal, rather like a baby crocodile but ... 57 _____

with a shorter head. It is quite harmless but doesn't look it. It is ... 71 _____

about six inches long and very slimy, with a greenish-grey skin on ... 83 _____

top and an orange-colored belly underneath. It is, in fact, an ... 94 _____

amphibian, which can live in or out of water. ... 103 _____

That evening Lavender went to the bottom of the garden ... 113 _____

determined to catch a newt. They are swiftly-moving animals and ... 123 _____

not easy to get hold of. She lay on the bank for a long time ... 138 _____

waiting patiently until she spotted a whopper. Then, using her ... 148 _____

school hat as a net, she swooped and caught it. She had lined her ... 162 _____

pencil-box with pond-weed ready to receive the creature, but she ... 172 _____

discovered that it was not easy to get the newt out of the hat and ... 187 _____

into the pencil-box. It wriggled and squirmed like quicksilver and, ... 197 _____

apart from that, the box was only just long enough to take it. ... 210 _____

Needs Work   1   2   3   4   5   Excellent
Paid attention to punctuation

Needs Work   1   2   3   4   5   Excellent
Sounded good

Total Words Read _____

Total Errors − _____

Correct WPM _____

27

Nonfiction

from *Snake's Daughter*
by Gail Hosking Gilberg

	Words Read	Miscues
While many fathers went to Vietnam once, my father kept going	11	_____
back until he died there.	16	_____
Once on one of his return trips home, he sat on the floor of	30	_____
our apartment wearing black Vietnamese pajamalike clothes,	37	_____
eating rice with chopsticks. While we ate meat loaf and mashed	48	_____
potatoes at the table, we listened to him speak about the men he	61	_____
left behind. I see now that the magical country of Vietnam had	73	_____
taken over his life, just like the war and the men at his side who	88	_____
became the reasons for fighting the war. Vietnam had a curious	99	_____
hold on my father I couldn't begin to understand then.	109	_____
On another visit home, he went with me to a high school	121	_____
football game dressed in his full military dress uniform. I had	132	_____
spent my life seeing him in uniform, and I knew he took it	145	_____
seriously. His pants were tucked into his polished black boots and	156	_____
all his insignia were aligned in their proper places. But that night	168	_____
as he stood on the bleachers dressed differently from anyone else,	179	_____
surrounded by civilians, I began to feel uncomfortable. It confused	189	_____
me. Had I known the right words then, I would have asked what	202	_____
it was all about: the war, the uniform, his always going away.	214	_____

Needs Work   1   2   3   4   5   Excellent
Paid attention to punctuation

Needs Work   1   2   3   4   5   Excellent
Sounded good

Total Words Read   _____

Total Errors   −_____

Correct WPM   _____

27

Nonfiction

from *Snake's Daughter*

by Gail Hosking Gilberg

	Words Read	Miscues

While many fathers went to Vietnam once, my father kept going | 11 | _____

back until he died there. | 16 | _____

Once on one of his return trips home, he sat on the floor of | 30 | _____

our apartment wearing black Vietnamese pajamalike clothes, | 37 | _____

eating rice with chopsticks. While we ate meat loaf and mashed | 48 | _____

potatoes at the table, we listened to him speak about the men he | 61 | _____

left behind. I see now that the magical country of Vietnam had | 73 | _____

taken over his life, just like the war and the men at his side who | 88 | _____

became the reasons for fighting the war. Vietnam had a curious | 99 | _____

hold on my father I couldn't begin to understand then. | 109 | _____

On another visit home, he went with me to a high school | 121 | _____

football game dressed in his full military dress uniform. I had | 132 | _____

spent my life seeing him in uniform, and I knew he took it | 145 | _____

seriously. His pants were tucked into his polished black boots and | 156 | _____

all his insignia were aligned in their proper places. But that night | 168 | _____

as he stood on the bleachers dressed differently from anyone else, | 179 | _____

surrounded by civilians, I began to feel uncomfortable. It confused | 189 | _____

me. Had I known the right words then, I would have asked what | 202 | _____

it was all about: the war, the uniform, his always going away. | 214 | _____

Needs Work   1   2   3   4   5   Excellent
Paid attention to punctuation

Needs Work   1   2   3   4   5   Excellent
Sounded good

Total Words Read _____

Total Errors − _____

Correct WPM _____

28
Nonfiction

from *Now Is Your Time!*
by Walter Dean Myers

	Words Read	Miscues

Using the pen name Iola, [Ida B. Wells] began writing for a | 12 | _____
religious publication called *The Evening Star.* Her well-written, | 20 | _____
lively articles soon attracted the attention of another religious | 29 | _____
publication, a weekly called *The Living Way.* | 36 | _____

    It was common practice at the time for newspapers to | 46 | _____
"borrow" articles from one another. Soon the work published with | 56 | _____
Iola's by-line was being reprinted in a number of African- | 66 | _____
American newspapers. Ida accepted a part-time job as a regular | 75 | _____
correspondent, receiving the fancy salary of one dollar a week. | 85 | _____

    Ida Wells wanted justice for her people and for women. She | 96 | _____
wasn't willing to take life on anyone else's terms. Freedom, she | 107 | _____
felt, meant control of one's own life. She fought for that control at | 120 | _____
every opportunity. In 1889 she was invited to write for a small | 132 | _____
paper owned by two men in Memphis: *Free Speech and Headlight.* | 143 | _____
One of the men was the editor, and the other the sales manager. | 156 | _____
Ida would be the only woman and the only employee without a | 168 | _____
title. It didn't sound very much like equality to the young woman. | 180 | _____
With money she had saved, she insisted on buying a share of the | 193 | _____
paper so that she would be an equal to the men. | 204 | _____

Needs Work   1 2 3 4 5 Excellent
_____
     Paid attention to punctuation

Needs Work   1 2 3 4 5 Excellent
_____
     Sounded good

Total Words Read   _____

Total Errors − _____

Correct WPM   _____

from *Now Is Your Time!*
by Walter Dean Myers

	Words Read	Miscues
Using the pen name Iola, [Ida B. Wells] began writing for a	12	_____
religious publication called *The Evening Star.* Her well-written,	20	_____
lively articles soon attracted the attention of another religious	29	_____
publication, a weekly called *The Living Way.*	36	_____
It was common practice at the time for newspapers to	46	_____
"borrow" articles from one another. Soon the work published with	56	_____
Iola's by-line was being reprinted in a number of African-	66	_____
American newspapers. Ida accepted a part-time job as a regular	75	_____
correspondent, receiving the fancy salary of one dollar a week.	85	_____
Ida Wells wanted justice for her people and for women. She	96	_____
wasn't willing to take life on anyone else's terms. Freedom, she	107	_____
felt, meant control of one's own life. She fought for that control at	120	_____
every opportunity. In 1889 she was invited to write for a small	132	_____
paper owned by two men in Memphis: *Free Speech and Headlight.*	143	_____
One of the men was the editor, and the other the sales manager.	156	_____
Ida would be the only woman and the only employee without a	168	_____
title. It didn't sound very much like equality to the young woman.	180	_____
With money she had saved, she insisted on buying a share of the	193	_____
paper so that she would be an equal to the men.	204	_____

Needs Work   1   2   3   4   5   Excellent
Paid attention to punctuation

Needs Work   1   2   3   4   5   Excellent
Sounded good

Total Words Read   _____

Total Errors −   _____

Correct WPM   _____

29

Nonfiction

Nellie Bly: Exposing the Truth

First Reading

	Words Read	Miscues

In 1888, Joseph Pulitzer, owner of the famous newspaper *The World,* asked Nellie Bly to write an article. He wanted her to investigate rumors of cruelty and neglect in the New York City insane asylum. The only way for Nellie to learn the truth was to become a patient herself. That meant she had to pretend she was crazy.

After being admitted to the hospital, Nellie soon learned that the staff did not pay much attention to any of the patients. She had expected medical care at the hospital to be minimal, but she was not prepared for the kind of heartless treatment that she saw all around her. Nellie was equally stunned by the filthy living conditions that prevailed throughout the hospital.

After a couple of days in that inhumane environment, Nellie was ready to get out. When she tried to explain to a doctor that she was not sick, he simply laughed and walked away.

Eventually, however, with the help of Pulitzer, Nellie was freed, and she began to work on her story. When she finished, Pulitzer ran it on the front page of *The World.* The story instantly created a scandal, stirring the public's concern for the mentally ill. Nellie was delighted that her newspaper article helped to change the city's attitude toward the mentally ill.

Words Read	Miscues
9	_____
22	_____
33	_____
45	_____
57	_____
59	_____
69	_____
82	_____
94	_____
106	_____
117	_____
123	_____
133	_____
147	_____
157	_____
167	_____
179	_____
192	_____
203	_____
213	_____
219	_____

Needs Work   1   2   3   4   5   Excellent
Paid attention to punctuation

Needs Work   1   2   3   4   5   Excellent
Sounded good

Total Words Read   _____

Total Errors   − _____

Correct WPM   _____

Nellie Bly: Exposing the Truth

	Words Read	Miscues

In 1888, Joseph Pulitzer, owner of the famous newspaper *The World,* asked Nellie Bly to write an article. He wanted her to investigate rumors of cruelty and neglect in the New York City insane asylum. The only way for Nellie to learn the truth was to become a patient herself. That meant she had to pretend she was crazy.

After being admitted to the hospital, Nellie soon learned that the staff did not pay much attention to any of the patients. She had expected medical care at the hospital to be minimal, but she was not prepared for the kind of heartless treatment that she saw all around her. Nellie was equally stunned by the filthy living conditions that prevailed throughout the hospital.

After a couple of days in that inhumane environment, Nellie was ready to get out. When she tried to explain to a doctor that she was not sick, he simply laughed and walked away.

Eventually, however, with the help of Pulitzer, Nellie was freed, and she began to work on her story. When she finished, Pulitzer ran it on the front page of *The World.* The story instantly created a scandal, stirring the public's concern for the mentally ill. Nellie was delighted that her newspaper article helped to change the city's attitude toward the mentally ill.

Words Read
9
22
33
45
57
59
69
82
94
106
117
123
133
147
157
167
179
192
203
213
219

Needs Work   1   2   3   4   5   Excellent
Paid attention to punctuation

Needs Work   1   2   3   4   5   Excellent
Sounded good

Total Words Read _____

Total Errors − _____

Correct WPM _____

30 from *Frankenstein*
by Mary Shelley

Fiction

	First Reading	
	Words Read	**Miscues**

	Words Read	Miscues
"One day, when I was oppressed by cold, I found a fire which	13	_____
had been left by some wandering beggars, and was overcome with	24	_____
delight at the warmth I experienced from it. In my joy I thrust my	38	_____
hand into the live embers, but quickly drew it out again with a cry	52	_____
of pain. How strange, I thought, that the same cause should	63	_____
produce such opposite effects! I examined the materials of the	73	_____
fire, and to my joy found it to be composed of wood. I quickly	87	_____
collected some branches; but they were wet, and would not burn.	98	_____
I was pained at this, and sat still watching the operation of the	111	_____
fire. The wet wood which I had placed near the heat dried, and	124	_____
itself became inflamed. I reflected on this; and, by touching the	135	_____
various branches, I discovered the cause, and busied myself in	145	_____
collecting a great quantity of wood, that I might dry it, and have a	159	_____
plentiful supply of fire. When night came on, and brought sleep	170	_____
with it, I was in the greatest fear lest my fire should be extinguished.	184	_____
I covered it carefully with dry wood and leaves, and placed wet	196	_____
branches upon it; and then, spreading my cloak, I lay on the	208	_____
ground, and sunk into sleep."	213	_____

Needs Work   1   2   3   4   5   Excellent
Paid attention to punctuation

Needs Work   1   2   3   4   5   Excellent
Sounded good

Total Words Read _____

Total Errors − _____

Correct WPM _____

from *Frankenstein*
by Mary Shelley

Second Reading

	Words Read	Miscues

"One day, when I was oppressed by cold, I found a fire which   13 _____

had been left by some wandering beggars, and was overcome with   24 _____

delight at the warmth I experienced from it. In my joy I thrust my   38 _____

hand into the live embers, but quickly drew it out again with a cry   52 _____

of pain. How strange, I thought, that the same cause should   63 _____

produce such opposite effects! I examined the materials of the   73 _____

fire, and to my joy found it to be composed of wood. I quickly   87 _____

collected some branches; but they were wet, and would not burn.   98 _____

I was pained at this, and sat still watching the operation of the   111 _____

fire. The wet wood which I had placed near the heat dried, and   124 _____

itself became inflamed. I reflected on this; and, by touching the   135 _____

various branches, I discovered the cause, and busied myself in   145 _____

collecting a great quantity of wood, that I might dry it, and have a   159 _____

plentiful supply of fire. When night came on, and brought sleep   170 _____

with it, I was in the greatest fear lest my fire should be extinguished.   184 _____

I covered it carefully with dry wood and leaves, and placed wet   196 _____

branches upon it; and then, spreading my cloak, I lay on the   208 _____

ground, and sunk into sleep."   213 _____

Needs Work   1 2 3 4 5   Excellent
Paid attention to punctuation

Needs Work   1 2 3 4 5   Excellent
Sounded good

Total Words Read _____

Total Errors − _____

Correct WPM _____

from *The Kidnapped Prince:*
The Life of Olaudah Equiano
by Olaudah Equiano
adapted by Ann Cameron

31 Nonfiction

First Reading

	Words Read	Miscues

In our village we were always ready for war. These wars were   12   _____

usually surprise attacks from strangers from another district who   21   _____

wanted to take prisoners or booty. Often, the attacks came when   32   _____

we were out of the village, working in the fields.   42   _____

    When we were afraid of the village being invaded, we guarded   53   _____

the streets leading to our houses with stakes struck into the   64   _____

ground. The exposed ends of the stakes had sharp points dipped   75   _____

in poison. The attacker who stepped on one would die.   85   _____

    It took a couple of hours to walk to our fields from the village.   99   _____

To prevent surprise attacks on the way to the fields, neighbors   110   _____

always walked together, carrying their hoes and axes and   119   _____

shovels—and their weapons too.   124   _____

    Our weapons were guns, bows and arrows, and broad two-   134   _____

edged swords. We also had spears, and also huge shields that   144   _____

could cover a man from head to foot.   152   _____

    Everybody was taught how to use these weapons, even the   162   _____

women. Our whole district was like a volunteer army. We all knew   174   _____

the warning signals, like the firing of a gun at night. When a   187   _____

signal came, we grabbed our weapons and rushed out of our   198   _____

houses to fight.   201   _____

Needs Work   1   2   3   4   5   Excellent
Paid attention to punctuation

Needs Work   1   2   3   4   5   Excellent
Sounded good

Total Words Read   _____

Total Errors   − _____

Correct WPM   _____

from *The Kidnapped Prince:*

The Life of Olaudah Equiano

by Olaudah Equiano

adapted by Ann Cameron

Second Reading

	Words Read	Miscues
In our village we were always ready for war. These wars were	12	_____
usually surprise attacks from strangers from another district who	21	_____
wanted to take prisoners or booty. Often, the attacks came when	32	_____
we were out of the village, working in the fields.	42	_____
When we were afraid of the village being invaded, we guarded	53	_____
the streets leading to our houses with stakes struck into the	64	_____
ground. The exposed ends of the stakes had sharp points dipped	75	_____
in poison. The attacker who stepped on one would die.	85	_____
It took a couple of hours to walk to our fields from the village.	99	_____
To prevent surprise attacks on the way to the fields, neighbors	110	_____
always walked together, carrying their hoes and axes and	119	_____
shovels—and their weapons too.	124	_____
Our weapons were guns, bows and arrows, and broad two-	134	_____
edged swords. We also had spears, and also huge shields that	144	_____
could cover a man from head to foot.	152	_____
Everybody was taught how to use these weapons, even the	162	_____
women. Our whole district was like a volunteer army. We all knew	174	_____
the warning signals, like the firing of a gun at night. When a	187	_____
signal came, we grabbed our weapons and rushed out of our	198	_____
houses to fight.	201	_____

Needs Work   1 2 3 4 5   Excellent
Paid attention to punctuation

Needs Work   1 2 3 4 5   Excellent
Sounded good

Total Words Read   _____

Total Errors   − _____

Correct WPM   _____

32

Nonfiction

from "Prime Time"
by Henry Louis Gates Jr.

First Reading

	Words Read	Miscues

The simple truth is that the civil rights era came late to   12   _____

Piedmont, even though it came early to our television set. We   23   _____

could watch what was going on Elsewhere on television, but the   34   _____

marches and sit-ins were as remote to us as, in other ways, was   47   _____

the all-colored world of *Amos and Andy*—a world full of black   59   _____

lawyers, black judges, black nurses, black doctors.   66   _____

Politics aside, though, we were starved for images of ourselves   76   _____

and searched TV to find them. Everybody, of course, watched   86   _____

sports, because Piedmont was a big sports town. Making the big   97   _____

leagues was like getting to Heaven, and everybody had hopes that   108   _____

they could, or a relative could. We'd watch the games day and   120   _____

night, and listen on radio to what we couldn't see. Everybody   131   _____

knew the latest scores, batting averages, rbi's, and stolen bases.   141   _____

Everybody knew the standings in the leagues, who could still win   152   _____

the pennant and how. Everybody liked the Dodgers because of   162   _____

Jackie Robinson, the same way everybody still voted Republican   171   _____

because of Abraham Lincoln. Sports on the mind, sports in the   182   _____

mind. The only thing to rival the Valley in fascination was the big-   195   _____

league baseball diamond.   197   _____

Needs Work   1 2 3 4 5   Excellent
Paid attention to punctuation

Needs Work   1 2 3 4 5   Excellent
Sounded good

Total Words Read _____

Total Errors − _____

Correct WPM _____

32

Nonfiction

from **"Prime Time"**

by Henry Louis Gates Jr.

	Words Read	Miscues

The simple truth is that the civil rights era came late to Piedmont, even though it came early to our television set. We could watch what was going on Elsewhere on television, but the marches and sit-ins were as remote to us as, in other ways, was the all-colored world of *Amos and Andy*—a world full of black lawyers, black judges, black nurses, black doctors.

Politics aside, though, we were starved for images of ourselves and searched TV to find them. Everybody, of course, watched sports, because Piedmont was a big sports town. Making the big leagues was like getting to Heaven, and everybody had hopes that they could, or a relative could. We'd watch the games day and night, and listen on radio to what we couldn't see. Everybody knew the latest scores, batting averages, rbi's, and stolen bases. Everybody knew the standings in the leagues, who could still win the pennant and how. Everybody liked the Dodgers because of Jackie Robinson, the same way everybody still voted Republican because of Abraham Lincoln. Sports on the mind, sports in the mind. The only thing to rival the Valley in fascination was the big-league baseball diamond.

Words read column:
12
23
34
47
59
66
76
86
97
108
120
131
141
152
162
171
182
195
197

Needs Work 1 2 3 4 5 Excellent
Paid attention to punctuation

Needs Work 1 2 3 4 5 Excellent
Sounded good

Total Words Read _____

Total Errors – _____

Correct WPM _____

33

Nonfiction

from *Dolphin Man:*
Exploring the World of Dolphins
by Laurence Pringle

First Reading

	Words Read	Miscues

∞∞∞

	Words Read	Miscues
Suddenly dolphins rose to the surface in groups of two and three	12	_____
on both sides of the boat. For an instant each dolphin revealed	24	_____
the top of its head and body, including its big dorsal (back) fin,	37	_____
before diving under again. And in that instant Randy Wells began	48	_____
to call out their names:	53	_____
"Pumpkin . . . Lightning . . . Merrily! And there's 55!"	59	_____
In another half minute the dolphins rose to breathe again.	69	_____
"There's 75 and her calf, and Killer and her calf," Randy called.	81	_____
Soon he had identified four more dolphins for a total of a	93	_____
dozen—about a tenth of the bottlenose dolphins that live in	104	_____
Sarasota Bay on Florida's central western coast.	111	_____
The boat followed the dolphins slowly as crew members took	121	_____
photographs of them and wrote down notes about their location	131	_____
and behavior. Randy and his crew discussed the identity of each	142	_____
dolphin, trying to make sure that they were correct.	151	_____
The photographs they took were not casual snapshots. Each	160	_____
year the research team led by Randy Wells takes twenty thousand	171	_____
photos of dolphins to record marks on their dorsal fins and other	183	_____
distinctive features that are clues to their identification. Each year	193	_____
they also capture some of the dolphins in nets to briefly study	205	_____
them more closely, and to collect blood samples and other	215	_____
information before they release them.	220	_____

Needs Work   1   2   3   4   5   Excellent
Paid attention to punctuation

Needs Work   1   2   3   4   5   Excellent
Sounded good

Total Words Read _____

Total Errors − _____

Correct WPM _____

from *Dolphin Man:*
Exploring the World of Dolphins
by Laurence Pringle

Suddenly dolphins rose to the surface in groups of two and three	12	_____
on both sides of the boat. For an instant each dolphin revealed	24	_____
the top of its head and body, including its big dorsal (back) fin,	37	_____
before diving under again. And in that instant Randy Wells began	48	_____
to call out their names:	53	_____
"Pumpkin . . . Lightning . . . Merrily! And there's 55!"	59	_____
In another half minute the dolphins rose to breathe again.	69	_____
"There's 75 and her calf, and Killer and her calf," Randy called.	81	_____
Soon he had identified four more dolphins for a total of a	93	_____
dozen—about a tenth of the bottlenose dolphins that live in	104	_____
Sarasota Bay on Florida's central western coast.	111	_____
The boat followed the dolphins slowly as crew members took	121	_____
photographs of them and wrote down notes about their location	131	_____
and behavior. Randy and his crew discussed the identity of each	142	_____
dolphin, trying to make sure that they were correct.	151	_____
The photographs they took were not casual snapshots. Each	160	_____
year the research team led by Randy Wells takes twenty thousand	171	_____
photos of dolphins to record marks on their dorsal fins and other	183	_____
distinctive features that are clues to their identification. Each year	193	_____
they also capture some of the dolphins in nets to briefly study	205	_____
them more closely, and to collect blood samples and other	215	_____
information before they release them.	220	_____

Needs Work   1   2   3   4   5   Excellent
Paid attention to punctuation

Needs Work   1   2   3   4   5   Excellent
Sounded good

Total Words Read   _____

Total Errors   −_____

Correct WPM   _____

34

Nonfiction

from *Marie Curie*
by Angela Bull

	Words Read	Miscues

[Pierre Curie] wanted the university simply to acknowledge the | 9 | _____
value of his work, and this they did not do. The French government, | 22 | _____
in 1902, actually offered him their highest decoration, the Legion | 32 | _____
of Honor, for his contribution to French science, but Pierre turned | 43 | _____
it down. "I do not feel the slightest need of being decorated," he | 56 | _____
wrote, "but I am in the greatest need of a laboratory." Still the | 69 | _____
academic world ignored him. | 73 | _____

The Curies were always short of money. Marie had no salary | 84 | _____
or grant, and Pierre's salary was so low that it was quickly | 96 | _____
swallowed up by their living expenses, and by the wages of the | 108 | _____
maid and nurse, who looked after the house and little Irene. | 119 | _____
There was none to spare for advancing their research, and so, to | 131 | _____
earn a bit more, Marie took a job in a girls' school, where she | 145 | _____
taught physics two days a week. She was an excellent teacher, one | 157 | _____
of the first to allow her pupils to try practical experiments. More | 169 | _____
importantly, the work gave her a regular break from the | 179 | _____
contaminated atmosphere of the shed—something which Pierre | 187 | _____
never had. But Marie did not realize her good fortune. She only | 199 | _____
grumbled at the time she wasted in preparing her lessons, | 209 | _____
teaching, and traveling to and fro. | 215 | _____

Needs Work   1 2 3 4 5   Excellent
Paid attention to punctuation

Needs Work   1 2 3 4 5   Excellent
Sounded good

Total Words Read   _____

Total Errors − _____

Correct WPM   _____

from *Marie Curie*
by Angela Bull

	Words Read	Miscues
[Pierre Curie] wanted the university simply to acknowledge the	9	_____
value of his work, and this they did not do. The French government,	22	_____
in 1902, actually offered him their highest decoration, the Legion	32	_____
of Honor, for his contribution to French science, but Pierre turned	43	_____
it down. "I do not feel the slightest need of being decorated," he	56	_____
wrote, "but I am in the greatest need of a laboratory." Still the	69	_____
academic world ignored him.	73	_____
The Curies were always short of money. Marie had no salary	84	_____
or grant, and Pierre's salary was so low that it was quickly	96	_____
swallowed up by their living expenses, and by the wages of the	108	_____
maid and nurse, who looked after the house and little Irene.	119	_____
There was none to spare for advancing their research, and so, to	131	_____
earn a bit more, Marie took a job in a girls' school, where she	145	_____
taught physics two days a week. She was an excellent teacher, one	157	_____
of the first to allow her pupils to try practical experiments. More	169	_____
importantly, the work gave her a regular break from the	179	_____
contaminated atmosphere of the shed—something which Pierre	187	_____
never had. But Marie did not realize her good fortune. She only	199	_____
grumbled at the time she wasted in preparing her lessons,	209	_____
teaching, and traveling to and fro.	215	_____

Needs Work   1   2   3   4   5   Excellent
Paid attention to punctuation

Needs Work   1   2   3   4   5   Excellent
Sounded good

Total Words Read   _____

Total Errors   − _____

Correct WPM   _____

35
Fiction

from **"An Occurrence at Owl Creek Bridge"**
by Ambrose Bierce

First Reading

	Words Read	Miscues

————

	Words Read	Miscues
By nightfall he was fatigued, footsore, famishing. The thought	9	_____
of his wife and children urged him on. At last he found a road	23	_____
which led him in what he knew to be the right direction. It was as	38	_____
wide and straight as a city street, yet it seemed untraveled. No	50	_____
fields bordered it, no dwelling anywhere. Not so much as the	61	_____
barking of a dog suggested human habitation. The black bodies of	72	_____
the trees formed a straight wall on both sides, terminating on the	84	_____
horizon in a point, like a diagram in a lesson in perspective.	96	_____
Overhead, as he looked up through this rift in the wood, shone	108	_____
great golden stars looking unfamiliar and grouped in strange	117	_____
constellations. He was sure they were arranged in some order	127	_____
which had a secret and malign significance. The wood on either	138	_____
side was full of singular noises, among which—once, twice, and	149	_____
again—he distinctly heard whispers in an unknown tongue.	158	_____
His neck was in pain and lifting his hand to it he found it	172	_____
horribly swollen. He knew that it had a circle of black where the	185	_____
rope had bruised it. His eyes felt congested; he could no longer	197	_____
close them. His tongue was swollen with thirst.	205	_____

Needs Work   1   2   3   4   5   Excellent
Paid attention to punctuation

Needs Work   1   2   3   4   5   Excellent
Sounded good

Total Words Read   _____

Total Errors − _____

Correct WPM   _____

35
Fiction

from "An Occurrence at Owl Creek Bridge"
by Ambrose Bierce

	Words Read	Miscues

By nightfall he was fatigued, footsore, famishing. The thought · 9 · _____
of his wife and children urged him on. At last he found a road · 23 · _____
which led him in what he knew to be the right direction. It was as · 38 · _____
wide and straight as a city street, yet it seemed untraveled. No · 50 · _____
fields bordered it, no dwelling anywhere. Not so much as the · 61 · _____
barking of a dog suggested human habitation. The black bodies of · 72 · _____
the trees formed a straight wall on both sides, terminating on the · 84 · _____
horizon in a point, like a diagram in a lesson in perspective. · 96 · _____
Overhead, as he looked up through this rift in the wood, shone · 108 · _____
great golden stars looking unfamiliar and grouped in strange · 117 · _____
constellations. He was sure they were arranged in some order · 127 · _____
which had a secret and malign significance. The wood on either · 138 · _____
side was full of singular noises, among which—once, twice, and · 149 · _____
again—he distinctly heard whispers in an unknown tongue. · 158 · _____

His neck was in pain and lifting his hand to it he found it · 172 · _____
horribly swollen. He knew that it had a circle of black where the · 185 · _____
rope had bruised it. His eyes felt congested; he could no longer · 197 · _____
close them. His tongue was swollen with thirst. · 205 · _____

Needs Work   1 2 3 4 5   Excellent
Paid attention to punctuation

Needs Work   1 2 3 4 5   Excellent
Sounded good

Total Words Read _____

Total Errors − _____

Correct WPM _____

36
Nonfiction

from *Charlotte Brontë and Jane Eyre*

by Stewart Ross

First Reading

	Words Read	Miscues

Patrick Brontë's duties as a clergyman kept him very busy. Even   11   ____

so, he always made time for his children. He ate breakfast and   23   ____

dinner with them. He guided their prayers and their reading—the   34   ____

whole family were great readers—and taught them history and   44   ____

geography. Whenever he could, he joined them for the high point   55   ____

of their day—lively romps over the sweeping moors.   64   ____

The natural landscape made a deep impression on the young   74   ____

Charlotte. Many years later she wrote how Jane Eyre, fleeing from   85   ____

the deceitful human world, found peace in the "golden desert" of   96   ____

the "spreading moor." Nature was steadfast and true. To the   106   ____

orphan Jane it was a "universal mother" that loved her when the   118   ____

world did not. There were times when Charlotte, Jane's creator,   128   ____

must have felt the same.   133   ____

Since all the Brontë children had powerful imaginations, there   142   ____

was never a dull moment when they played together. Their   152   ____

favorite indoor pursuits were making up games and stories and   162   ____

performing plays they had written. The central character was   171   ____

always the Duke of Wellington, Charlotte's hero, who had   180   ____

defeated Napoleon at Waterloo. If her brother or sisters ever   190   ____

suggested replacing the Duke with Napoleon or Julius Caesar,   199   ____

there would be an argument. Then Patrick would have to come   210   ____

out of his study to sort things out.   218   ____

Needs Work   1   2   3   4   5   Excellent
Paid attention to punctuation

Needs Work   1   2   3   4   5   Excellent
Sounded good

Total Words Read   _____

Total Errors   − _____

Correct WPM   _____

from *Charlotte Brontë
and Jane Eyre*

by Stewart Ross

	Words Read	Miscues

Patrick Brontë's duties as a clergyman kept him very busy. Even so, he always made time for his children. He ate breakfast and dinner with them. He guided their prayers and their reading—the whole family were great readers—and taught them history and geography. Whenever he could, he joined them for the high point of their day—lively romps over the sweeping moors.

The natural landscape made a deep impression on the young Charlotte. Many years later she wrote how Jane Eyre, fleeing from the deceitful human world, found peace in the "golden desert" of the "spreading moor." Nature was steadfast and true. To the orphan Jane it was a "universal mother" that loved her when the world did not. There were times when Charlotte, Jane's creator, must have felt the same.

Since all the Brontë children had powerful imaginations, there was never a dull moment when they played together. Their favorite indoor pursuits were making up games and stories and performing plays they had written. The central character was always the Duke of Wellington, Charlotte's hero, who had defeated Napoleon at Waterloo. If her brother or sisters ever suggested replacing the Duke with Napoleon or Julius Caesar, there would be an argument. Then Patrick would have to come out of his study to sort things out.

Words Read
11
23
34
44
55
64
74
85
96
106
118
128
133
142
152
162
171
180
190
199
210
218

Needs Work   1 2 3 4 5   Excellent
Paid attention to punctuation

Needs Work   1 2 3 4 5   Excellent
Sounded good

Total Words Read _____

Total Errors − _____

Correct WPM _____

from *Robots Rising*

by Carol Sonenklar

Nonfiction

	Words Read	Miscues

Even though scientists can program a robot to do difficult · 10 · _____

tasks or even specific complex mathematics, they cannot make a · 20 · _____

robot walk upright, like a human—it's too hard. When you walk, · 32 · _____

you must continuously balance yourself to adjust to whatever · 41 · _____

bumps in the road or obstacles you encounter. Balancing is an · 52 · _____

exquisitely complicated ability: your brain must give out a steady · 62 · _____

stream of instructions to your nervous system and then to the · 73 · _____

muscles of your bones, and your vision, for starters. · 82 · _____

In the mid-1980s, Rodney Brooks, a famous roboticist at MIT, · 92 · _____

noticed that insects and spiders, who don't have very large or · 103 · _____

complicated brains, could move over any terrain, find food for · 113 · _____

themselves, and hide from predators. Their six or eight legs gave · 124 · _____

them great stability and mobility; their antennae sensed obstacles · 133 · _____

and danger. But they did all this without a large central brain · 145 · _____

"telling" them what to do, so they didn't "learn" this behavior as · 157 · _____

we do. · 159 · _____

And Brooks thought: Why not build a robot that has the brain · 171 · _____

of an insect? · 174 · _____

So he did. In so doing, Brooks changed the way a lot of people · 188 · _____

think robots should be built. Six-legged *Genghis,* created in 1988 · 198 · _____

in Brooks's Mobot Laboratory at MIT, was the first walking insect · 209 · _____

robot. Instead of a central nervous system, his robot had various · 220 · _____

interconnected motion and light sensors located all over its body. · 230 · _____

Needs Work 1 2 3 4 5 Excellent
Paid attention to punctuation

Needs Work 1 2 3 4 5 Excellent
Sounded good

Total Words Read _____

Total Errors − _____

Correct WPM _____

from *Robots Rising*
by Carol Sonenklar

	Words Read	Miscues

Even though scientists can program a robot to do difficult | 10 | _____
tasks or even specific complex mathematics, they cannot make a | 20 | _____
robot walk upright, like a human—it's too hard. When you walk, | 32 | _____
you must continuously balance yourself to adjust to whatever | 41 | _____
bumps in the road or obstacles you encounter. Balancing is an | 52 | _____
exquisitely complicated ability: your brain must give out a steady | 62 | _____
stream of instructions to your nervous system and then to the | 73 | _____
muscles of your bones, and your vision, for starters. | 82 | _____

In the mid-1980s, Rodney Brooks, a famous roboticist at MIT, | 92 | _____
noticed that insects and spiders, who don't have very large or | 103 | _____
complicated brains, could move over any terrain, find food for | 113 | _____
themselves, and hide from predators. Their six or eight legs gave | 124 | _____
them great stability and mobility; their antennae sensed obstacles | 133 | _____
and danger. But they did all this without a large central brain | 145 | _____
"telling" them what to do, so they didn't "learn" this behavior as | 157 | _____
we do. | 159 | _____

And Brooks thought: Why not build a robot that has the brain | 171 | _____
of an insect? | 174 | _____

So he did. In so doing, Brooks changed the way a lot of people | 188 | _____
think robots should be built. Six-legged *Genghis,* created in 1988 | 198 | _____
in Brooks's Mobot Laboratory at MIT, was the first walking insect | 209 | _____
robot. Instead of a central nervous system, his robot had various | 220 | _____
interconnected motion and light sensors located all over its body. | 230 | _____

Needs Work 1 2 3 4 5 Excellent
Paid attention to punctuation

Needs Work 1 2 3 4 5 Excellent
Sounded good

Total Words Read _____

Total Errors − _____

Correct WPM _____

38
Fiction

from *Only Earth and Sky Last Forever*
by Nathaniel Benchley

	Words Read	Miscues

When I got near the trap I led my pony into the woods and 14 _____
tethered him where he couldn't be seen from above. Then, 24 _____
working only by the light of the stars, I moved the last bits of sod 39 _____
and grass near the hole, took the pieces of jackrabbit out of my 52 _____
sack and put them on top of the covering, and then climbed into 65 _____
the hole. Lying on my back, I pulled the sod in place over my 79 _____
head, getting my eyes and mouth full of dirt as I did. . . . 91 _____

I lay on my back, silently praying for the strength I was going 104 _____
to need, and I slowly became aware of the coming of day. Little 117 _____
chinks of gray showed through the covering over my head, then 128 _____
the gray turned to blue, and the blue to bright white. I could see 142 _____
small patches of sky, which was a help, and I only hoped that any 156 _____
eagle up there wouldn't be able to see me as well. Time passed, 169 _____
and as the sun began to warm the ground I could smell the 182 _____
jackrabbit, even through the turf and grass. I wondered if it would 194 _____
attract a coyote or a wolf, and figured I'd have to take care of that 209 _____
situation if and when it happened. 215 _____

Needs Work   1 2 3 4 5   Excellent
Paid attention to punctuation

Needs Work   1 2 3 4 5   Excellent
Sounded good

Total Words Read _____

Total Errors − _____

Correct WPM _____

38

Fiction

from *Only Earth and Sky Last Forever*

by Nathaniel Benchley

	Words Read	Miscues

When I got near the trap I led my pony into the woods and | 14 | _____
tethered him where he couldn't be seen from above. Then, | 24 | _____
working only by the light of the stars, I moved the last bits of sod | 39 | _____
and grass near the hole, took the pieces of jackrabbit out of my | 52 | _____
sack and put them on top of the covering, and then climbed into | 65 | _____
the hole. Lying on my back, I pulled the sod in place over my | 79 | _____
head, getting my eyes and mouth full of dirt as I did. . . . | 91 | _____

I lay on my back, silently praying for the strength I was going | 104 | _____
to need, and I slowly became aware of the coming of day. Little | 117 | _____
chinks of gray showed through the covering over my head, then | 128 | _____
the gray turned to blue, and the blue to bright white. I could see | 142 | _____
small patches of sky, which was a help, and I only hoped that any | 156 | _____
eagle up there wouldn't be able to see me as well. Time passed, | 169 | _____
and as the sun began to warm the ground I could smell the | 182 | _____
jackrabbit, even through the turf and grass. I wondered if it would | 194 | _____
attract a coyote or a wolf, and figured I'd have to take care of that | 209 | _____
situation if and when it happened. | 215 | _____

Needs Work   1   2   3   4   5   Excellent
Paid attention to punctuation

Needs Work   1   2   3   4   5   Excellent
Sounded good

Total Words Read _____

Total Errors − _____

Correct WPM _____

76

39
Fiction

from *Drifting Snow:*
An Arctic Search
by James Houston

	Words Read	Miscues
There was no landing strip on Nesak, a rough, rocky island named	12	_____
with the Inuit word meaning "hat" because the island was shaped	23	_____
just like a hat.	27	_____
The four families dwelling above the beach continued to live	37	_____
their nomadic lives in spite of modern times. They moved with	48	_____
every season, following the animals—birds, fish, and caribou—	57	_____
animals that supported them and allowed them to stay alive. In	68	_____
winter and in early spring, these hunting families lived on this	79	_____
island. Later, they would pull their boats on sleds behind their	90	_____
snowmobiles across the great expanse of sea ice to the mouth of	102	_____
the Kokjuak River on Baffin Island. It would be a long day's	114	_____
journey for them, but the plane had taken only a few minutes	126	_____
to cross.	128	_____
Inside their winter tent, Poota pulled on his silver-spotted,	137	_____
knee-length, outer sealskin pants, and then his best navy-blue	146	_____
parka with red-and-white braid near his hips and around his	156	_____
wrists. Setting his many-colored woolen hat upon his head, then	166	_____
pulling up his hood, he hurried through the tent's low door. Any	178	_____
day when they had visitors was a very special day.	188	_____
As the strong metal skis of the bright red plane touched down	200	_____
on the snow, he watched the plane bounce, then hop, then skim	212	_____
roughly over the hard white drifts.	218	_____

Needs Work   1   2   3   4   5   Excellent
Paid attention to punctuation

Needs Work   1   2   3   4   5   Excellent
Sounded good

Total Words Read _____

Total Errors − _____

Correct WPM _____

from *Drifting Snow:*

An Arctic Search

by James Houston

	Words Read	Miscues

There was no landing strip on Nesak, a rough, rocky island named | 12 | _____

with the Inuit word meaning "hat" because the island was shaped | 23 | _____

just like a hat. | 27 | _____

The four families dwelling above the beach continued to live | 37 | _____

their nomadic lives in spite of modern times. They moved with | 48 | _____

every season, following the animals—birds, fish, and caribou— | 57 | _____

animals that supported them and allowed them to stay alive. In | 68 | _____

winter and in early spring, these hunting families lived on this | 79 | _____

island. Later, they would pull their boats on sleds behind their | 90 | _____

snowmobiles across the great expanse of sea ice to the mouth of | 102 | _____

the Kokjuak River on Baffin Island. It would be a long day's | 114 | _____

journey for them, but the plane had taken only a few minutes | 126 | _____

to cross. | 128 | _____

Inside their winter tent, Poota pulled on his silver-spotted, | 137 | _____

knee-length, outer sealskin pants, and then his best navy-blue | 146 | _____

parka with red-and-white braid near his hips and around his | 156 | _____

wrists. Setting his many-colored woolen hat upon his head, then | 166 | _____

pulling up his hood, he hurried through the tent's low door. Any | 178 | _____

day when they had visitors was a very special day. | 188 | _____

As the strong metal skis of the bright red plane touched down | 200 | _____

on the snow, he watched the plane bounce, then hop, then skim | 212 | _____

roughly over the hard white drifts. | 218 | _____

Needs Work   1 2 3 4 5   Excellent
Paid attention to punctuation

Needs Work   1 2 3 4 5   Excellent
Sounded good

Total Words Read _____

Total Errors − _____

Correct WPM _____

40
Fiction

from *Tales from Watership Down*
by Richard Adams

	Words Read	Miscues
The Down lay empty all around, and the breeze brought no scent	12	_____
of [enemies] but only the familiar smells of juniper and thyme.	23	_____
After the days of restriction in the frost-bound burrows, the	33	_____
spaciousness was exhilarating, and several of the rabbits began	42	_____
leaping and chasing one another almost like hares. Hazel felt the	53	_____
release as fully as anyone and joined happily in a mock fight with	66	_____
Speedwell and Silver in and out of the junipers. Running away	77	_____
from Speedwell, he ran down the steep north-facing slope, pulled	87	_____
up sharply in front of a thornbush and lost his balance, rolling	99	_____
over against a sodden tussock.	104	_____
Picking himself up, Hazel, with a shock, saw a dog racing	115	_____
uphill toward him, yapping with excitement. It was a smooth-	125	_____
haired fox terrier, white with brown patches, soaking wet and	134	_____
muddy from the ditches and furrows down below. Hazel turned,	144	_____
breaking into his limping run, but even as he put on his best	157	_____
speed he knew that he was not fast enough; the dog was gaining	170	_____
on him. Desperately he changed direction, dodging one way and	180	_____
another, and as he did he felt the dog's breath panting closer,	192	_____
almost on top of him.	197	_____

Needs Work   1   2   3   4   5   Excellent
Paid attention to punctuation

Needs Work   1   2   3   4   5   Excellent
Sounded good

Total Words Read   _____

Total Errors   − _____

Correct WPM   _____

from *Tales from Watership Down*
by Richard Adams

Second Reading

	Words Read	Miscues

The Down lay empty all around, and the breeze brought no scent | 12 | _____

of [enemies] but only the familiar smells of juniper and thyme. | 23 | _____

After the days of restriction in the frost-bound burrows, the | 33 | _____

spaciousness was exhilarating, and several of the rabbits began | 42 | _____

leaping and chasing one another almost like hares. Hazel felt the | 53 | _____

release as fully as anyone and joined happily in a mock fight with | 66 | _____

Speedwell and Silver in and out of the junipers. Running away | 77 | _____

from Speedwell, he ran down the steep north-facing slope, pulled | 87 | _____

up sharply in front of a thornbush and lost his balance, rolling | 99 | _____

over against a sodden tussock. | 104 | _____

    Picking himself up, Hazel, with a shock, saw a dog racing | 115 | _____

uphill toward him, yapping with excitement. It was a smooth- | 125 | _____

haired fox terrier, white with brown patches, soaking wet and | 134 | _____

muddy from the ditches and furrows down below. Hazel turned, | 144 | _____

breaking into his limping run, but even as he put on his best | 157 | _____

speed he knew that he was not fast enough; the dog was gaining | 170 | _____

on him. Desperately he changed direction, dodging one way and | 180 | _____

another, and as he did he felt the dog's breath panting closer, | 192 | _____

almost on top of him. | 197 | _____

Needs Work   1   2   3   4   5   Excellent
Paid attention to punctuation

Needs Work   1   2   3   4   5   Excellent
Sounded good

Total Words Read   _____

Total Errors   − _____

Correct WPM   _____

41

Fiction

from "The Golden Darters"
by Elizabeth Winthrop

First Reading

	Words Read	Miscues

I was twelve years old when my father started tying flies. It | 12 | _____
was an odd habit for a man who had just undergone a serious | 25 | _____
operation on his upper back, but, as he remarked to my mother | 37 | _____
one night, at least it gave him a world over which he had some | 51 | _____
control. | 52 | _____

The family grew used to seeing him hunched down close to his | 64 | _____
tying vise, hackle pliers in one hand, thread bobbin in the other. | 76 | _____
We began to bandy about strange phrases—foxy quills, bodkins, | 86 | _____
peacock hurl. Father's corner of the living room was off limits to | 98 | _____
the maid with the voracious and destructive vacuum cleaner. Who | 108 | _____
knew what precious bit of calf's tail or rabbit fur would be sucked | 121 | _____
away never to be seen again. | 127 | _____

Because of my father's illness, we had gone up to our summer | 139 | _____
cottage on the lake in New Hampshire a month early. None of my | 152 | _____
gang of friends ever came till the end of July, so in the beginning | 166 | _____
of that summer I hung around home watching my father as he | 178 | _____
fussed with the flies. I was the only child he allowed to stand near | 192 | _____
him while he worked. | 196 | _____

Needs Work   1   2   3   4   5   Excellent
Paid attention to punctuation

Needs Work   1   2   3   4   5   Excellent
Sounded good

Total Words Read _____

Total Errors − _____

Correct WPM _____

from "The Golden Darters"

by Elizabeth Winthrop

I was twelve years old when my father started tying flies. It	12
was an odd habit for a man who had just undergone a serious	25
operation on his upper back, but, as he remarked to my mother	37
one night, at least it gave him a world over which he had some	51
control.	52
The family grew used to seeing him hunched down close to his	64
tying vise, hackle pliers in one hand, thread bobbin in the other.	76
We began to bandy about strange phrases—foxy quills, bodkins,	86
peacock hurl. Father's corner of the living room was off limits to	98
the maid with the voracious and destructive vacuum cleaner. Who	108
knew what precious bit of calf's tail or rabbit fur would be sucked	121
away never to be seen again.	127
Because of my father's illness, we had gone up to our summer	139
cottage on the lake in New Hampshire a month early. None of my	152
gang of friends ever came till the end of July, so in the beginning	166
of that summer I hung around home watching my father as he	178
fussed with the flies. I was the only child he allowed to stand near	192
him while he worked.	196

Needs Work   1 2 3 4 5   Excellent
Paid attention to punctuation

Needs Work   1 2 3 4 5   Excellent
Sounded good

Total Words Read _____

Total Errors − _____

Correct WPM _____

42

Nonfiction

from *The Moon of the Alligators*
by Jean Craighead George

First Reading

Words Read	Miscues

Two eyes poked above the still water. Each iris was silver-   11 _____

yellow and each pupil black and narrow. They were the eyes of   22 _____

the alligator of Sawgrass Hole, who was floating like a log on the   35 _____

surface of the water as she watched for food. She saw the blue sky   49 _____

above her, and because her eyes were on the top and to the rear   63 _____

of her head, she saw all the way behind her to the tall cypress   77 _____

trees. Their limbs spread like silver wires above a tangle of sweet 89 _____

bay and buttonbushes.   92 _____

    The alligator did not move, but watched and waited even   102 _____

though hunger gnawed her belly. She had eaten little since June,   113 _____

when the rainy season had flooded her home and the prey she   125 _____

fed upon had swum away. Now her sense of seasonal rhythm told   137 _____

her that the afternoon's cloudless sky meant the end of the rains   149 _____

and hurricanes, and the return of the wildlife to her water hole.   161 _____

The moon of October was the beginning of southern Florida's dry   172 _____

season. The water level would fall. The fish, frogs, turtles, and   183 _____

birds would come back to Sawgrass Hole, where she lived. They   194 _____

would be followed by the herons and ibis, egrets, . . . [and] water 205 _____

turkeys, and she would eat well once more.   213 _____

Needs Work   1 2 3 4 5   Excellent
Paid attention to punctuation

Needs Work   1 2 3 4 5   Excellent
Sounded good

Total Words Read _____

Total Errors − _____

Correct WPM _____

from *The Moon of the Alligators*

by Jean Craighead George

	Words Read	Miscues

Two eyes poked above the still water. Each iris was silver-yellow and each pupil black and narrow. They were the eyes of the alligator of Sawgrass Hole, who was floating like a log on the surface of the water as she watched for food. She saw the blue sky above her, and because her eyes were on the top and to the rear of her head, she saw all the way behind her to the tall cypress trees. Their limbs spread like silver wires above a tangle of sweet bay and buttonbushes.

The alligator did not move, but watched and waited even though hunger gnawed her belly. She had eaten little since June, when the rainy season had flooded her home and the prey she fed upon had swum away. Now her sense of seasonal rhythm told her that the afternoon's cloudless sky meant the end of the rains and hurricanes, and the return of the wildlife to her water hole. The moon of October was the beginning of southern Florida's dry season. The water level would fall. The fish, frogs, turtles, and birds would come back to Sawgrass Hole, where she lived. They would be followed by the herons and ibis, egrets, . . . [and] water turkeys, and she would eat well once more.

Words Read
11
22
35
49
63
77
89
92
102
113
125
137
149
161
172
183
194
205
213

Needs Work   1   2   3   4   5   Excellent

Paid attention to punctuation

Needs Work   1   2   3   4   5   Excellent

Sounded good

Total Words Read   _____

Total Errors   − _____

Correct WPM   _____

from *The Samurai and the Long-Nosed Devils*

Fiction

by Lensey Namioka

First Reading

	Words Read	Miscues

Breathless after crossing the mountain pass, the two travelers — 9

stood for a moment and looked down on the dark gray roofs of — 22

Miyako. The capital city was situated in a small plain surrounded — 33

on three sides by mountains. On this July afternoon, the heat lay — 45

trapped in the city as if in a large bowl. The air vibrated with the — 60

heat, and to the tired eyes of the travelers, the roof tiles seemed to — 74

be jumping up and down. — 79

The men each wore two swords thrust into their sashes, — 89

marking them as samurai. Their kimonos were of silk and had — 100

once been even elegant, but they were now torn and white with — 112

dust. On their feet the travelers wore straw sandals nearly falling — 123

apart from hard use. Still, the two men carried themselves with — 134

the unconscious haughtiness of the warrior class, although it was — 144

clear from their shabby condition that they were *ronin,* or — 154

unemployed samurai. — 156

As they made their way down into the city, Matsuzo, the — 167

younger of the two ronin, removed his large basket-shaped hat — 177

and wiped his face with his sleeve. "How much money do we — 189

have left?" he asked. — 193

Zenta, his companion, groped inside the front of his kimono — 203

and brought out a few coins. "I'm afraid this is all we have." — 216

Matsuzo's face fell. "Well, it should be enough for a bath, — 227

at least." — 229

Needs Work   1   2   3   4   5   Excellent
Paid attention to punctuation

Needs Work   1   2   3   4   5   Excellent
Sounded good

Total Words Read _____

Total Errors − _____

Correct WPM _____

43

Fiction

from *The Samurai and the Long-Nosed Devils*

by Lensey Namioka

	Words Read	Miscues

Breathless after crossing the mountain pass, the two travelers stood for a moment and looked down on the dark gray roofs of Miyako. The capital city was situated in a small plain surrounded on three sides by mountains. On this July afternoon, the heat lay trapped in the city as if in a large bowl. The air vibrated with the heat, and to the tired eyes of the travelers, the roof tiles seemed to be jumping up and down.

The men each wore two swords thrust into their sashes, marking them as samurai. Their kimonos were of silk and had once been even elegant, but they were now torn and white with dust. On their feet the travelers wore straw sandals nearly falling apart from hard use. Still, the two men carried themselves with the unconscious haughtiness of the warrior class, although it was clear from their shabby condition that they were *ronin,* or unemployed samurai.

As they made their way down into the city, Matsuzo, the younger of the two ronin, removed his large basket-shaped hat and wiped his face with his sleeve. "How much money do we have left?" he asked.

Zenta, his companion, groped inside the front of his kimono and brought out a few coins. "I'm afraid this is all we have."

Matsuzo's face fell. "Well, it should be enough for a bath, at least."

Words Read
9
22
33
45
60
74
79
89
100
112
123
134
144
154
156
167
177
189
193
203
216
227
229

Needs Work   1   2   3   4   5   Excellent

Paid attention to punctuation

Needs Work   1   2   3   4   5   Excellent

Sounded good

Total Words Read _____

Total Errors − _____

Correct WPM _____

44

Nonfiction

The Development of Ballet

First Reading

	Words Read	Miscues

Ballet began in the royal courts during the Renaissance. At   10 _____

that time it became common for kings and queens, as well as   22 _____

other nobility, to participate in pageants that included music,   31 _____

poetry, and dance. As these entertainments moved from the   40 _____

Italian courts to the French ones, court ladies began participating   50 _____

in them. Though their long dresses prevented much movement,   59 _____

they were able to perform elaborate walking patterns. It was not   70 _____

until the 1600s that women dancers shortened their skirts,   79 _____

changed to flat shoes, and began doing some of the leaps and   91 _____

turns performed by men.   95 _____

It was also in the 1600s that professional ballet began. The   106 _____

five basic foot positions from which all ballet steps begin were   117 _____

finalized. In the late 1700s another important change occurred.   126 _____

Ballet began to tell a story on its own. By the early 1800s   139 _____

dancers learned to rise on their toes to make it appear that   151 _____

they were floating.   154 _____

Classical ballet as we know it today was influenced primarily   164 _____

by Russian dancing. One of the most influential figures of the   175 _____

early 20th century was Sergei Diaghilev. His dance company   184 _____

brought a new energy and excitement to ballet. One of his chief   196 _____

assistants, George Balanchine, went on to found the New York   206 _____

City Ballet in 1948 and to influence new generations of dancers.   217 _____

Needs Work   1   2   3   4   5   Excellent
Paid attention to punctuation

Needs Work   1   2   3   4   5   Excellent
Sounded good

Total Words Read _____

Total Errors − _____

Correct WPM _____

The Development of Ballet

Ballet began in the royal courts during the Renaissance. At   10 _____
that time it became common for kings and queens, as well as   22 _____
other nobility, to participate in pageants that included music,   31 _____
poetry, and dance. As these entertainments moved from the   40 _____
Italian courts to the French ones, court ladies began participating   50 _____
in them. Though their long dresses prevented much movement,   59 _____
they were able to perform elaborate walking patterns. It was not   70 _____
until the 1600s that women dancers shortened their skirts,   79 _____
changed to flat shoes, and began doing some of the leaps and   91 _____
turns performed by men.   95 _____

It was also in the 1600s that professional ballet began. The   106 _____
five basic foot positions from which all ballet steps begin were   117 _____
finalized. In the late 1700s another important change occurred.   126 _____
Ballet began to tell a story on its own. By the early 1800s   139 _____
dancers learned to rise on their toes to make it appear that   151 _____
they were floating.   154 _____

Classical ballet as we know it today was influenced primarily   164 _____
by Russian dancing. One of the most influential figures of the   175 _____
early 20th century was Sergei Diaghilev. His dance company   184 _____
brought a new energy and excitement to ballet. One of his chief   196 _____
assistants, George Balanchine, went on to found the New York   206 _____
City Ballet in 1948 and to influence new generations of dancers.   217 _____

Needs Work   1   2   3   4   5   Excellent
Paid attention to punctuation

Needs Work   1   2   3   4   5   Excellent
Sounded good

Total Words Read _____

Total Errors − _____

Correct WPM _____

45

Nonfiction

from *To the Top of the World:*
Adventures with Arctic Wolves
by Jim Brandenburg

First Reading

	Words Read	Miscues

Wolves are probably one of the most social animals outside of the   12   _____

primates. The success of the pack depends strongly on a highly   23   _____

developed system of communication with neighboring packs as   31   _____

well as between individual pack members. Smell, vision, and   40   _____

hearing play crucial roles in such communication.   47   _____

The most well-known form of communication wolves use is   56   _____

their howl. Howling begins at a very early age. Within weeks after   68   _____

emerging from the den, the pups [turn] their tiny snouts to the   80   _____

sky right alongside their parents.   85   _____

I was often able to watch and listen to a songfest by the whole   99   _____

pack. Each had his or her distinctive voice and a preferred range   111   _____

of notes. [A wolf I called] Midback, for instance, had a high-   123   _____

pitched, almost whiny cry, whereas Left Shoulder would howl in   132   _____

the lower octaves.   135   _____

Whatever their preferred notes, however, one thing was   143   _____

certain. Every wolf avoided hitting the same note as any of its   155   _____

packmates. When this happened by accident, one of the voices   165   _____

would frantically shuffle about until discord could be achieved   174   _____

once again. This phenomenon apparently has evolved to suit the   184   _____

scattered distribution of the Arctic wolves across an unfriendly   193   _____

environment, not always in safe numbers. With as many different   203   _____

tones as possible in its howling, a pack can give the impression of   216   _____

greater size and can intimidate possible intruders.   223   _____

Needs Work   1   2   3   4   5   Excellent
Paid attention to punctuation

Needs Work   1   2   3   4   5   Excellent
Sounded good

Total Words Read   _____

Total Errors   − _____

Correct WPM   _____

45

Nonfiction

from *To the Top of the World:*
Adventures with Arctic Wolves
by Jim Brandenburg

	Words Read	Miscues

Wolves are probably one of the most social animals outside of the | 12 | _____
primates. The success of the pack depends strongly on a highly | 23 | _____
developed system of communication with neighboring packs as | 31 | _____
well as between individual pack members. Smell, vision, and | 40 | _____
hearing play crucial roles in such communication. | 47 | _____

    The most well-known form of communication wolves use is | 56 | _____
their howl. Howling begins at a very early age. Within weeks after | 68 | _____
emerging from the den, the pups [turn] their tiny snouts to the | 80 | _____
sky right alongside their parents. | 85 | _____

    I was often able to watch and listen to a songfest by the whole | 99 | _____
pack. Each had his or her distinctive voice and a preferred range | 111 | _____
of notes. [A wolf I called] Midback, for instance, had a high- | 123 | _____
pitched, almost whiny cry, whereas Left Shoulder would howl in | 132 | _____
the lower octaves. | 135 | _____

    Whatever their preferred notes, however, one thing was | 143 | _____
certain. Every wolf avoided hitting the same note as any of its | 155 | _____
packmates. When this happened by accident, one of the voices | 165 | _____
would frantically shuffle about until discord could be achieved | 174 | _____
once again. This phenomenon apparently has evolved to suit the | 184 | _____
scattered distribution of the Arctic wolves across an unfriendly | 193 | _____
environment, not always in safe numbers. With as many different | 203 | _____
tones as possible in its howling, a pack can give the impression of | 216 | _____
greater size and can intimidate possible intruders. | 223 | _____

Needs Work   1 2 3 4 5   Excellent
Paid attention to punctuation

Needs Work   1 2 3 4 5   Excellent
Sounded good

Total Words Read _____

Total Errors – _____

Correct WPM _____

46

Fiction

from *Hidden Trail*
by Jim Kjelgaard

	Words Read	Miscues

He turned south, toward the big bend of the river, [his dog] | 12 | _____
Buckles scouting along first on one side of him, then the other. | 24 | _____

    As he approached the bend, motion on the river brought him | 35 | _____
to a sudden stop. | 39 | _____

    Four or five hundred yards away, eleven great gray wolves | 49 | _____
trotted across the frozen river, emerged from the willows on the | 60 | _____
far side, and continued at right angles to the southward direction | 71 | _____
in which Jase was traveling. They knew he was there and Jase | 83 | _____
knew they knew, but they did not hurry. They seemed to sense | 95 | _____
that the human and dog were too far away to be any threat. | 108 | _____

    Jase took out his camera, focused his telephoto lens on the | 119 | _____
lazily traveling pack, and shot a sequence. He knew even before | 130 | _____
he started shooting that he would not get a good sequence under | 142 | _____
the hazy light conditions, but that was unimportant. He wanted it | 153 | _____
for the record, for he was certain that the pack had come into the | 167 | _____
valley of the Mary to prey on the wintering elk. | 177 | _____

    As he sheathed his camera again, Jase became aware that there | 188 | _____
had been a shift in the wind direction. For three days it had | 201 | _____
blown out of the north, but now it was coming from the east, and | 215 | _____
was definitely warmer. He glanced up at the sky. | 224 | _____

Needs Work   1   2   3   4   5   Excellent
Paid attention to punctuation

Needs Work   1   2   3   4   5   Excellent
Sounded good

Total Words Read _____

Total Errors − _____

Correct WPM _____

from *Hidden Trail*
by Jim Kjelgaard

	Words Read	Miscues
He turned south, toward the big bend of the river, [his dog]	12	_____
Buckles scouting along first on one side of him, then the other.	24	_____
As he approached the bend, motion on the river brought him	35	_____
to a sudden stop.	39	_____
Four or five hundred yards away, eleven great gray wolves	49	_____
trotted across the frozen river, emerged from the willows on the	60	_____
far side, and continued at right angles to the southward direction	71	_____
in which Jase was traveling. They knew he was there and Jase	83	_____
knew they knew, but they did not hurry. They seemed to sense	95	_____
that the human and dog were too far away to be any threat.	108	_____
Jase took out his camera, focused his telephoto lens on the	119	_____
lazily traveling pack, and shot a sequence. He knew even before	130	_____
he started shooting that he would not get a good sequence under	142	_____
the hazy light conditions, but that was unimportant. He wanted it	153	_____
for the record, for he was certain that the pack had come into the	167	_____
valley of the Mary to prey on the wintering elk.	177	_____
As he sheathed his camera again, Jase became aware that there	188	_____
had been a shift in the wind direction. For three days it had	201	_____
blown out of the north, but now it was coming from the east, and	215	_____
was definitely warmer. He glanced up at the sky.	224	_____

Needs Work 1 2 3 4 5 Excellent
Paid attention to punctuation

Needs Work 1 2 3 4 5 Excellent
Sounded good

Total Words Read _____

Total Errors − _____

Correct WPM _____

47

Nonfiction

from *Mary Cassatt:*

Portrait of an American Impressionist

by Tom Streissguth

While still in school, Mary [Cassatt] decided that she would	10
make a living on her own as a painter. After graduating from high	23
school, she had to spend a long time working up enough courage	35
to break the news to her father. She would have to choose the	48
right words and find him in the right mood. She knew he might	61
not take it very well.	66
She would have to return to Europe. To learn to paint, that	78
was where one must study, and the best way to study was to copy	92
museum pictures and work in artists' studios in France, Spain, or	103
Italy. She would learn from professional artists and meet other	113
students. She would travel. Europe wasn't like Philadelphia; there	122
were beautiful sculptures in the streets and squares. There were	132
paintings displayed in the windows of small galleries and on the	143
walls of vast cathedrals. People in Europe had art surrounding	153
them—they talked about art like Americans talked about money!	163
Robert Cassatt was patient and understanding. He listened to	172
his daughter. He knew that Mary had talent, but even so, talented	184
young ladies should not be bothered with careers. They especially	194
did not work as painters. Art could be a hobby they might try, but	208
only when their real duties, as wives and as mothers, allowed	219
them time.	221

Needs Work   1   2   3   4   5   Excellent
_____
        Paid attention to punctuation

Needs Work   1   2   3   4   5   Excellent
_____
            Sounded good

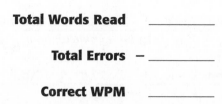

Total Words Read _____

Total Errors − _____

Correct WPM _____

from *Mary Cassatt:*
Portrait of an American Impressionist
by Tom Streissguth

Words Read	Miscues

While still in school, Mary [Cassatt] decided that she would make a living on her own as a painter. After graduating from high school, she had to spend a long time working up enough courage to break the news to her father. She would have to choose the right words and find him in the right mood. She knew he might not take it very well.

She would have to return to Europe. To learn to paint, that was where one must study, and the best way to study was to copy museum pictures and work in artists' studios in France, Spain, or Italy. She would learn from professional artists and meet other students. She would travel. Europe wasn't like Philadelphia; there were beautiful sculptures in the streets and squares. There were paintings displayed in the windows of small galleries and on the walls of vast cathedrals. People in Europe had art surrounding them—they talked about art like Americans talked about money!

Robert Cassatt was patient and understanding. He listened to his daughter. He knew that Mary had talent, but even so, talented young ladies should not be bothered with careers. They especially did not work as painters. Art could be a hobby they might try, but only when their real duties, as wives and as mothers, allowed them time.

Words Read
10
23
35
48
61
66
78
92
103
113
122
132
143
153
163
172
184
194
208
219
221

Needs Work   1   2   3   4   5   Excellent
Paid attention to punctuation

Needs Work   1   2   3   4   5   Excellent
Sounded good

Total Words Read _____

Total Errors − _____

Correct WPM _____

from *Taking Sides*
by Gary Soto

Fiction

	Words Read	Miscues

When he had arrived in the new neighborhood, Lincoln had — 10 — _____

liked the peacefulness of sprinklers hissing on green lawns and — 20 — _____

the sycamores that lined the street. He liked the splashes of — 31 — _____

flowers and neatly piled firewood. He liked the hedges where jays — 42 — _____

built scrawny nests and bickered when cats slithered too close. — 52 — _____

The people seemed distant, but that was fine with him. It was — 64 — _____

better than the loud cars that raced up and down his old block. It — 78 — _____

was better than littered streets and graffiti-covered walls. . . . — 86 — _____

Now, three months later, Lincoln was having second thoughts. — 95 — _____

He missed his old school and its mural of brown, black, and — 107 — _____

yellow kids linking arms in friendship. He had liked Franklin — 117 — _____

Junior High, tough as it was, with its fights in the hallways and in — 131 — _____

the noisy cafeteria. He had liked to walk among brown faces and — 143 — _____

stand with the Vietnamese and Korean kids. He missed his — 153 — _____

friends, especially his number-one man, Tony Contreras, whom he — 162 — _____

had known forever, even before first grade when Tony accidentally — 172 — _____

knocked out Lincoln's front baby teeth going down the slide. And — 183 — _____

he missed Vicky. They had parted on bad terms, but Lincoln felt — 195 — _____

that if he could speak with her everything would turn out OK. — 207 — _____

Needs Work   1   2   3   4   5   Excellent
Paid attention to punctuation

Needs Work   1   2   3   4   5   Excellent
Sounded good

Total Words Read   _____

Total Errors − _____

Correct WPM   _____

from *Taking Sides*
by Gary Soto

When he had arrived in the new neighborhood, Lincoln had — **10**

liked the peacefulness of sprinklers hissing on green lawns and — **20**

the sycamores that lined the street. He liked the splashes of — **31**

flowers and neatly piled firewood. He liked the hedges where jays — **42**

built scrawny nests and bickered when cats slithered too close. — **52**

The people seemed distant, but that was fine with him. It was — **64**

better than the loud cars that raced up and down his old block. It — **78**

was better than littered streets and graffiti-covered walls. . . . — **86**

Now, three months later, Lincoln was having second thoughts. — **95**

He missed his old school and its mural of brown, black, and — **107**

yellow kids linking arms in friendship. He had liked Franklin — **117**

Junior High, tough as it was, with its fights in the hallways and in — **131**

the noisy cafeteria. He had liked to walk among brown faces and — **143**

stand with the Vietnamese and Korean kids. He missed his — **153**

friends, especially his number-one man, Tony Contreras, whom he — **162**

had known forever, even before first grade when Tony accidentally — **172**

knocked out Lincoln's front baby teeth going down the slide. And — **183**

he missed Vicky. They had parted on bad terms, but Lincoln felt — **195**

that if he could speak with her everything would turn out OK. — **207**

Needs Work   1   2   3   4   5   Excellent
Paid attention to punctuation

Needs Work   1   2   3   4   5   Excellent
Sounded good

Total Words Read _____

Total Errors − _____

Correct WPM _____

from *April and the Dragon Lady*
by Lensey Namioka

Fiction

First Reading

	Words Read	Miscues

When I came home from school on Monday and opened the   11   _____

front door, a cloud of delectable smells hit me in the face.   23   _____

These days Grandma still insisted on doing most of the   33   _____

cooking, but she prepared simple meals—rice and a couple of   44   _____

stir-fried dishes of meat and vegetables. On weekends I took her   55   _____

to Chinatown and stocked up on a variety of Chinese convenience   66   _____

foods like sausages, pickled eggs, cans of vegetables already   75   _____

sliced and cooked, and packages of frozen steamed breads   84   _____

and savory pastries.   87   _____

But the smells today were a sign of a major cooking effort. I   100   _____

was immediately worried that Grandma might be working too   109   _____

hard. However energetic, she was after all seventy years old. In   120   _____

China, seventy-year-old women were supported on both sides   128   _____

when they got up and tottered around, especially in the old days   140   _____

when they had bound feet.   145   _____

There was something unfamiliar, too, about the combination   153   _____

of spices. Was she trying out a new dish? I could smell star anise,   167   _____

Sichuan pickle, and sesame oil. I had to swallow hard, because I   179   _____

was literally drooling.   182   _____

After putting my backpack down, I turned to the living   192   _____

room and found a little boy there sitting on the couch,   203   _____

watching television.   205   _____

Needs Work   1   2   3   4   5   Excellent

Paid attention to punctuation

Needs Work   1   2   3   4   5   Excellent

Sounded good

Total Words Read _____

Total Errors − _____

Correct WPM _____

from *April and the Dragon Lady*
by Lensey Namioka

	Words Read	Miscues

When I came home from school on Monday and opened the — 11

front door, a cloud of delectable smells hit me in the face. — 23

These days Grandma still insisted on doing most of the — 33

cooking, but she prepared simple meals—rice and a couple of — 44

stir-fried dishes of meat and vegetables. On weekends I took her — 55

to Chinatown and stocked up on a variety of Chinese convenience — 66

foods like sausages, pickled eggs, cans of vegetables already — 75

sliced and cooked, and packages of frozen steamed breads — 84

and savory pastries. — 87

But the smells today were a sign of a major cooking effort. I — 100

was immediately worried that Grandma might be working too — 109

hard. However energetic, she was after all seventy years old. In — 120

China, seventy-year-old women were supported on both sides — 128

when they got up and tottered around, especially in the old days — 140

when they had bound feet. — 145

There was something unfamiliar, too, about the combination — 153

of spices. Was she trying out a new dish? I could smell star anise, — 167

Sichuan pickle, and sesame oil. I had to swallow hard, because I — 179

was literally drooling. — 182

After putting my backpack down, I turned to the living — 192

room and found a little boy there sitting on the couch, — 203

watching television. — 205

Needs Work 1 2 3 4 5 Excellent
Paid attention to punctuation

Needs Work 1 2 3 4 5 Excellent
Sounded good

Total Words Read _____

Total Errors − _____

Correct WPM _____

50
Nonfiction

from *Isaac Bashevis Singer:*
The Life of a Storyteller
by Lila Perl

First Reading

	Words Read	Miscues

⚭⚭⚭

There were both bad and good aspects to Isaac's job as a | 12 | _____
proofreader. The work, as he'd expected, was monotonous, hard | 21 | _____
on the eyes, and sometimes exasperating. The writers who | 30 | _____
contributed to *Literary Pages* often handed in material that was | 40 | _____
not quite ready to be set in print. It was Isaac's job to check | 54 | _____
through the Yiddish printers' proofs for errors and to correct | 64 | _____
them. The stories themselves, Isaac often felt, were poorly | 73 | _____
conceived and written, and he wondered why the editors bought | 83 | _____
them. Isaac harbored dreams of producing some publishable | 91 | _____
writing of his own. His head buzzed with ideas, but who would | 103 | _____
ever buy a story from him? | 109 | _____

Though Isaac's days were now mainly full of toil and poverty, | 120 | _____
there *were* several advantages to living on his own as a young | 132 | _____
man in Warsaw. Being away from his family and having given up | 144 | _____
his religious studies, Isaac ceased to dress as a religious Jew. Gone | 156 | _____
were his earlocks and his Hasidic garments, for he now led a | 168 | _____
worldly life. As an employee of a literary journal, Isaac was | 179 | _____
admitted to the Warsaw Writers' Club, and this became for him | 190 | _____
the closest thing to a home. At the Writers' Club, one could find a | 204 | _____
warm corner in winter in which to sit and read, do some writing, | 217 | _____
or play chess. | 220 | _____

Needs Work   1 2 3 4 5   Excellent
Paid attention to punctuation

Needs Work   1 2 3 4 5   Excellent
Sounded good

Total Words Read   _____

Total Errors   − _____

Correct WPM   _____

from *Isaac Bashevis Singer:*
The Life of a Storyteller
by Lila Perl

	Words Read	Miscues

There were both bad and good aspects to Isaac's job as a
proofreader. The work, as he'd expected, was monotonous, hard
on the eyes, and sometimes exasperating. The writers who
contributed to *Literary Pages* often handed in material that was
not quite ready to be set in print. It was Isaac's job to check
through the Yiddish printers' proofs for errors and to correct
them. The stories themselves, Isaac often felt, were poorly
conceived and written, and he wondered why the editors bought
them. Isaac harbored dreams of producing some publishable
writing of his own. His head buzzed with ideas, but who would
ever buy a story from him?

Though Isaac's days were now mainly full of toil and poverty,
there *were* several advantages to living on his own as a young
man in Warsaw. Being away from his family and having given up
his religious studies, Isaac ceased to dress as a religious Jew. Gone
were his earlocks and his Hasidic garments, for he now led a
worldly life. As an employee of a literary journal, Isaac was
admitted to the Warsaw Writers' Club, and this became for him
the closest thing to a home. At the Writers' Club, one could find a
warm corner in winter in which to sit and read, do some writing,
or play chess.

Line	Words Read
	12
	21
	30
	40
	54
	64
	73
	83
	91
	103
	109
	120
	132
	144
	156
	168
	179
	190
	204
	217
	220

Needs Work   1 2 3 4 5   Excellent
Paid attention to punctuation

Needs Work   1 2 3 4 5   Excellent
Sounded good

Total Words Read _____

Total Errors − _____

Correct WPM _____

The Seneca Falls Convention

51
Nonfiction

	Words Read	Miscues

In 1848 Seneca Falls, located in upstate New York, was a rural — 12 _____

town. In July, a notice in the local newspaper announced that — 23 _____

public meetings would be held in the local chapel on the subject — 35 _____

of women's rights. Only a few dozen people were expected to — 46 _____

attend. To the astonishment of the organizers, hundreds of — 55 _____

women showed up. — 58 _____

One of the meetings' organizers was Elizabeth Cady Stanton. — 67 _____

As she rose to speak, she did not know how well she would — 80 _____

present her ideas. She had never spoken in public before. — 90 _____

She read from the Declaration of Sentiments and Resolutions, — 99 _____

a document in which several complaints and demands were — 108 _____

presented regarding the rights of women. One demand was for — 118 _____

the right to vote. — 122 _____

"'Resolved,'" Stanton read, "'that it is the duty of the women — 133 _____

of this country to secure to themselves their sacred right to the — 145 _____

elective franchise.'" — 147 _____

As expected, there was opposition to the resolution. Guided by — 157 _____

Stanton, the resolution finally passed—by a narrow margin. — 166 _____

The public reacted to the resolution with outrage. Newspaper — 175 _____

editorials accused the women of trying to tear down the nation. — 186 _____

One paper accused them of trying to upset "existing institutions — 196 _____

and [seeking to] overturn all the social relations of life." — 206 _____

Despite the outcry, important changes had been set in motion. — 216 _____

Needs Work   1   2   3   4   5   Excellent
Paid attention to punctuation

Needs Work   1   2   3   4   5   Excellent
Sounded good

Total Words Read _____

Total Errors − _____

Correct WPM _____

The Seneca Falls Convention

	Words Read	Miscues

In 1848 Seneca Falls, located in upstate New York, was a rural   12   _____

town. In July, a notice in the local newspaper announced that   23   _____

public meetings would be held in the local chapel on the subject   35   _____

of women's rights. Only a few dozen people were expected to   46   _____

attend. To the astonishment of the organizers, hundreds of   55   _____

women showed up.   58   _____

One of the meetings' organizers was Elizabeth Cady Stanton.   67   _____

As she rose to speak, she did not know how well she would   80   _____

present her ideas. She had never spoken in public before.   90   _____

She read from the Declaration of Sentiments and Resolutions,   99   _____

a document in which several complaints and demands were   108   _____

presented regarding the rights of women. One demand was for   118   _____

the right to vote.   122   _____

"'Resolved,'" Stanton read, "'that it is the duty of the women   133   _____

of this country to secure to themselves their sacred right to the   145   _____

elective franchise.'"   147   _____

As expected, there was opposition to the resolution. Guided by   157   _____

Stanton, the resolution finally passed—by a narrow margin.   166   _____

The public reacted to the resolution with outrage. Newspaper   175   _____

editorials accused the women of trying to tear down the nation.   186   _____

One paper accused them of trying to upset "existing institutions   196   _____

and [seeking to] overturn all the social relations of life."   206   _____

Despite the outcry, important changes had been set in motion.   216   _____

Needs Work   1   2   3   4   5   Excellent
Paid attention to punctuation

Needs Work   1   2   3   4   5   Excellent
Sounded good

Total Words Read   _____

Total Errors   − _____

Correct WPM   _____

52 from *No Promises in the Wind*

by Irene Hunt

Fiction

	Words Read	Miscues

I stared at the faded paper on the wall in front of me without   14   _____

really seeing it until I became conscious of the yellowed figures of   26   _____

cowboys riding their broncs in precise paths from baseboard to   36   _____

ceiling. My mother had allowed me to select that paper five years   48   _____

before when I was no older than [my younger brother] Joey, and I   61   _____

had held out for cowboys and broncs, scorning Mom's preference   71   _____

for pots of flowers or bright colored birds. I studied the horses   83   _____

and their daredevil riders for a long time as if they mattered. They   96   _____

didn't, of course, but concentrating on them kept me awake.   106   _____

Finally I [fully awakened]. My paper route didn't mean much   116   _____

money, but it was important. Dad had been out of work for eight   129   _____

months, and only the day before, my sister had received notice   140   _____

of a cut-back in personnel which cost her the clerking job she'd   152   _____

had for nearly a year. Every few pennies counted in our family;   164   _____

a job was a job, and to risk losing it by being late was out of   180   _____

the question.   182   _____

It was dark in the kitchen when I went downstairs, but I could   195   _____

see the outline of my mother's figure as she stood at the stove.   208   _____

Needs Work   1   2   3   4   5   Excellent
Paid attention to punctuation

Needs Work   1   2   3   4   5   Excellent
Sounded good

Total Words Read _____

Total Errors − _____

Correct WPM _____

from *No Promises in the Wind*

by Irene Hunt

	Words Read	Miscues

I stared at the faded paper on the wall in front of me without | 14
really seeing it until I became conscious of the yellowed figures of | 26
cowboys riding their broncs in precise paths from baseboard to | 36
ceiling. My mother had allowed me to select that paper five years | 48
before when I was no older than [my younger brother] Joey, and I | 61
had held out for cowboys and broncs, scorning Mom's preference | 71
for pots of flowers or bright colored birds. I studied the horses | 83
and their daredevil riders for a long time as if they mattered. They | 96
didn't, of course, but concentrating on them kept me awake. | 106

Finally I [fully awakened]. My paper route didn't mean much | 116
money, but it was important. Dad had been out of work for eight | 129
months, and only the day before, my sister had received notice | 140
of a cut-back in personnel which cost her the clerking job she'd | 152
had for nearly a year. Every few pennies counted in our family; | 164
a job was a job, and to risk losing it by being late was out of | 180
the question. | 182

It was dark in the kitchen when I went downstairs, but I could | 195
see the outline of my mother's figure as she stood at the stove. | 208

Needs Work   1 2 3 4 5   Excellent
Paid attention to punctuation

Needs Work   1 2 3 4 5   Excellent
Sounded good

Total Words Read _____

Total Errors − _____

Correct WPM _____

53

Nonfiction

from *Thomas Edison:*

American Inventor

by Roselyn and Ray Eldon Hiebert

First Reading

	Words Read	Miscues

Acrid smells frequently poured out of the basement workshop | 9 | _____
as Tom [Edison] plunged into the world of chemistry. The cellar | 20 | _____
became littered with the remains of chemicals and bottles, and his | 31 | _____
parents grew concerned that something serious might happen. | 39 | _____
Finally his mother told him to clean up the laboratory and quit | 51 | _____
his experiments, but the boy was so grief-stricken that she | 61 | _____
relented. She made a rigid rule, however, that he must lock the | 73 | _____
cellar when he was not working, so that nobody could get in and | 86 | _____
cause an accident. | 89 | _____

For hours, Tom locked himself in the dark room beneath the | 100 | _____
house, puttering with batteries and chemical formulas instead of | 109 | _____
playing outdoors. When his mother called him for his tutoring, he | 120 | _____
worked with her on other studies, but he never did well in | 132 | _____
English composition. Even later, when he was nineteen, his letters | 142 | _____
home showed a sad lack of proficiency in writing. | 151 | _____

Tom's mother understood how he loved to experiment and she | 161 | _____
sometimes let him work throughout the day with his wires, test | 172 | _____
tubes, and gases. | 175 | _____

"My mother was the making of me," Edison later said. "She | 186 | _____
understood me. She let me follow my bent." | 194 | _____

Needs Work 1 2 3 4 5 Excellent
Paid attention to punctuation

Needs Work 1 2 3 4 5 Excellent
Sounded good

Total Words Read _____

Total Errors – _____

Correct WPM _____

from *Thomas Edison:*
American Inventor
by Roselyn and Ray Eldon Hiebert

	Words Read	Miscues

Acrid smells frequently poured out of the basement workshop
as Tom [Edison] plunged into the world of chemistry. The cellar
became littered with the remains of chemicals and bottles, and his
parents grew concerned that something serious might happen.
Finally his mother told him to clean up the laboratory and quit
his experiments, but the boy was so grief-stricken that she
relented. She made a rigid rule, however, that he must lock the
cellar when he was not working, so that nobody could get in and
cause an accident.

For hours, Tom locked himself in the dark room beneath the
house, puttering with batteries and chemical formulas instead of
playing outdoors. When his mother called him for his tutoring, he
worked with her on other studies, but he never did well in
English composition. Even later, when he was nineteen, his letters
home showed a sad lack of proficiency in writing.

Tom's mother understood how he loved to experiment and she
sometimes let him work throughout the day with his wires, test
tubes, and gases.

"My mother was the making of me," Edison later said. "She
understood me. She let me follow my bent."

Words Read	Miscues
9	_____
20	_____
31	_____
39	_____
51	_____
61	_____
73	_____
86	_____
89	_____
100	_____
109	_____
120	_____
132	_____
142	_____
151	_____
161	_____
172	_____
175	_____
186	_____
194	_____

Needs Work   1   2   3   4   5   Excellent
Paid attention to punctuation

Needs Work   1   2   3   4   5   Excellent
Sounded good

Total Words Read _____

Total Errors − _____

Correct WPM _____

54

Fiction

from *Buried Onions*
by Gary Soto

	Words Read	Miscues

He walked over to the hill and stood on it, his shadow like a — 14 — _____

flagpole behind him. He threw back his head as he drained his — 26 — _____

coffee and then jumped up and down, smiling, puffs of dirt rising — 38 — _____

around his work boots. I knew he was imagining how his yard — 50 — _____

would bloom and his neighbors would stop to admire it. In mid- — 62 — _____

May it was a nice dream. — 67 — _____

"I'm going to plant a birch," he said as he climbed down. — 79 — _____

I asked him about the tree, and he said it was the kind of tree — 94 — _____

that grows in New England, especially along the shady twists and — 105 — _____

turns of babbling brooks. I couldn't imagine such a place. I — 116 — _____

couldn't imagine a place where the sun didn't gnaw at my eyes, — 128 — _____

gnaw with its bright hunger so that every other minute my pupils — 140 — _____

had to adjust themselves. I closed my eyes for a brief second and — 153 — _____

wondered what this tree was doing in Fresno. No rivers spun — 164 — _____

through our town, and it certainly didn't look like New England, — 175 — _____

though we did have one barren subdivision called Connecticut — 184 — _____

Meadows. I had to laugh at that because most of the people who — 197 — _____

lived there were Korean. — 201 — _____

Mr. Stiles said to dig where he'd been standing. — 210 — _____

Needs Work 1 2 3 4 5 Excellent
Paid attention to punctuation

Needs Work 1 2 3 4 5 Excellent
Sounded good

Total Words Read _____

Total Errors − _____

Correct WPM _____

from *Buried Onions*
by Gary Soto

He walked over to the hill and stood on it, his shadow like a
flagpole behind him. He threw back his head as he drained his
coffee and then jumped up and down, smiling, puffs of dirt rising
around his work boots. I knew he was imagining how his yard
would bloom and his neighbors would stop to admire it. In mid–
May it was a nice dream.

"I'm going to plant a birch," he said as he climbed down.

I asked him about the tree, and he said it was the kind of tree
that grows in New England, especially along the shady twists and
turns of babbling brooks. I couldn't imagine such a place. I
couldn't imagine a place where the sun didn't gnaw at my eyes,
gnaw with its bright hunger so that every other minute my pupils
had to adjust themselves. I closed my eyes for a brief second and
wondered what this tree was doing in Fresno. No rivers spun
through our town, and it certainly didn't look like New England,
though we did have one barren subdivision called Connecticut
Meadows. I had to laugh at that because most of the people who
lived there were Korean.

Mr. Stiles said to dig where he'd been standing.

Words Read
14
26
38
50
62
67
79
94
105
116
128
140
153
164
175
184
197
201
210

Needs Work   1 2 3 4 5   Excellent
Paid attention to punctuation

Needs Work   1 2 3 4 5   Excellent
Sounded good

Total Words Read _____

Total Errors − _____

Correct WPM _____

55
Fiction

from *Petrouchka:*
The Story of the Ballet
retold by Vivian Werner

	Words Read	Miscues

It was Shrove Tuesday, the day of the annual Shrovetide Fair, — 11 — _____

and the people of old St. Petersburg were in a festive mood. They — 24 — _____

gathered in the town square, laughing and joking, waving and — 34 — _____

shouting greetings to one another, slapping one another on — 43 — _____

the back. — 45 — _____

They all knew that Lent would begin the very next day. There — 57 — _____

would be no feasting after that—no dancing, no merrymaking at — 68 — _____

all until Easter, many long weeks away. — 75 — _____

Snow floated down in feathery flakes on that Shrove Tuesday, — 85 — _____

over a hundred and fifty years ago. It settled alike on the — 97 — _____

kerchiefed heads of peasant women and the elegant coats of — 107 — _____

gentlemen. It drifted over the graceful yellow and pink and pale — 118 — _____

blue buildings that ringed the square, and coated the colorfully — 128 — _____

decorated booths inside it. — 132 — _____

Early as it was, those scarlet and green and gold booths had — 144 — _____

been set up even earlier. Now the old women bustled about, — 155 — _____

busily setting out their wares. Shivering, they pulled their fringed — 165 — _____

shawls closer around their shoulders to ward off the cold. — 175 — _____

One pudgy little woman in a long, bright apron festooned her — 186 — _____

booth with fat ropes of sausage. Another polished the big brass — 197 — _____

samovar in which she would brew her fragrant tea. — 206 — _____

Needs Work   1   2   3   4   5   Excellent
Paid attention to punctuation

Needs Work   1   2   3   4   5   Excellent
Sounded good

Total Words Read _____

Total Errors − _____

Correct WPM _____

from *Petrouchka:*
The Story of the Ballet
retold by Vivian Werner

	Words Read	Miscues

It was Shrove Tuesday, the day of the annual Shrovetide Fair, — 11 — _____

and the people of old St. Petersburg were in a festive mood. They — 24 — _____

gathered in the town square, laughing and joking, waving and — 34 — _____

shouting greetings to one another, slapping one another on — 43 — _____

the back. — 45 — _____

They all knew that Lent would begin the very next day. There — 57 — _____

would be no feasting after that—no dancing, no merrymaking at — 68 — _____

all until Easter, many long weeks away. — 75 — _____

Snow floated down in feathery flakes on that Shrove Tuesday, — 85 — _____

over a hundred and fifty years ago. It settled alike on the — 97 — _____

kerchiefed heads of peasant women and the elegant coats of — 107 — _____

gentlemen. It drifted over the graceful yellow and pink and pale — 118 — _____

blue buildings that ringed the square, and coated the colorfully — 128 — _____

decorated booths inside it. — 132 — _____

Early as it was, those scarlet and green and gold booths had — 144 — _____

been set up even earlier. Now the old women bustled about, — 155 — _____

busily setting out their wares. Shivering, they pulled their fringed — 165 — _____

shawls closer around their shoulders to ward off the cold. — 175 — _____

One pudgy little woman in a long, bright apron festooned her — 186 — _____

booth with fat ropes of sausage. Another polished the big brass — 197 — _____

samovar in which she would brew her fragrant tea. — 206 — _____

Needs Work   1   2   3   4   5   Excellent
Paid attention to punctuation

Needs Work   1   2   3   4   5   Excellent
Sounded good

Total Words Read   _____

Total Errors − _____

Correct WPM   _____

56

Nonfiction

"I Will Fight No More Forever"

First Reading

	Words Read	Miscues

For centuries the Nez Perce had called Oregon's Wallowa   9   _____

Valley home. However, by 1877 the U.S. government had ordered   19   _____

the Nez Perce to move to a reservation in Idaho. Chief Joseph   31   _____

resisted but finally, to protect the lives of his people, he began   43   _____

leading them toward the Idaho reservation. Along the way, some   53   _____

of his men rebelled and killed a group of settlers. Chief Joseph   65   _____

knew the Army would retaliate, and so he changed course, seeking   76   _____

the safety of Canada.   80   _____

For months, the outnumbered Nez Perce warriors evaded or   89   _____

fought the Army troops that pursued them. Finally, the Army   99   _____

caught the group by surprise, surrounding them. After five days   109   _____

Chief Joseph surrendered. The Nez Perce had traveled over one   119   _____

thousand miles and were about forty miles from their destination.   129   _____

At the surrender Chief Joseph gave a now-famous speech that   139   _____

includes these words: "The little children are freezing to death.   149   _____

My people, some of them, have run away to the hills and have no   163   _____

blankets, no food. No one knows where they are—perhaps   173   _____

freezing to death. I want to have time to look for my children and   187   _____

see how many I can find. Maybe I shall find them among the   200   _____

dead. Hear me, my chiefs. I am tired; my heart is sick and sad.   214   _____

From where the sun now stands, I will fight no more forever."   226   _____

Needs Work   1   2   3   4   5   Excellent
Paid attention to punctuation

Needs Work   1   2   3   4   5   Excellent
Sounded good

Total Words Read _____

Total Errors – _____

Correct WPM _____

"I Will Fight No More Forever"

Second Reading

	Words Read	Miscues

For centuries the Nez Perce had called Oregon's Wallowa — 9 _____

Valley home. However, by 1877 the U.S. government had ordered — 19 _____

the Nez Perce to move to a reservation in Idaho. Chief Joseph — 31 _____

resisted but finally, to protect the lives of his people, he began — 43 _____

leading them toward the Idaho reservation. Along the way, some — 53 _____

of his men rebelled and killed a group of settlers. Chief Joseph — 65 _____

knew the Army would retaliate, and so he changed course, seeking — 76 _____

the safety of Canada. — 80 _____

For months, the outnumbered Nez Perce warriors evaded or — 89 _____

fought the Army troops that pursued them. Finally, the Army — 99 _____

caught the group by surprise, surrounding them. After five days — 109 _____

Chief Joseph surrendered. The Nez Perce had traveled over one — 119 _____

thousand miles and were about forty miles from their destination. — 129 _____

At the surrender Chief Joseph gave a now-famous speech that — 139 _____

includes these words: "The little children are freezing to death. — 149 _____

My people, some of them, have run away to the hills and have no — 163 _____

blankets, no food. No one knows where they are—perhaps — 173 _____

freezing to death. I want to have time to look for my children and — 187 _____

see how many I can find. Maybe I shall find them among the — 200 _____

dead. Hear me, my chiefs. I am tired; my heart is sick and sad. — 214 _____

From where the sun now stands, I will fight no more forever." — 226 _____

Needs Work   1 2 3 4 5   Excellent
Paid attention to punctuation

Needs Work   1 2 3 4 5   Excellent
Sounded good

Total Words Read _____

Total Errors   − _____

Correct WPM _____

57
Fiction

from "Brother Death"
by Sherwood Anderson

	Words Read	Miscues

There was a back porch to the Grey house . . . and from the **12** _____
porch steps a path led down to a stone springhouse. A spring **24** _____
came out of the ground just there, and there was a tiny stream **37** _____
that went along the edge of a field, past two large barns and out **51** _____
across a meadow to a creek—called a "branch" in Virginia, and **63** _____
the two trees stood close together beyond the springhouse and **73** _____
the fence. **75** _____

They were [strong] trees, their roots down in the rich, always **86** _____
damp soil, and one of them had a great limb that came down **99** _____
near the ground, so that Ted and Mary could climb into it and **112** _____
out another limb into its brother tree, and in the fall, when other **125** _____
trees, at the front and side of the house, had shed their leaves, **138** _____
blood-red leaves still clung to the two oaks. They were like dry **150** _____
blood on gray days, but on other days, when the sun came out, **163** _____
the trees flamed against distant hills. The leaves clung, whispering **173** _____
and talking when the wind blew, so that the trees themselves **184** _____
seemed carrying on a conversation. **189** _____

John Grey had decided he would have the trees cut. At first it **202** _____
was not a very definite decision. "I think I'll have them cut," he **215** _____
announced. **216** _____

"But why?" his wife asked. **221** _____

Needs Work 1 2 3 4 5 Excellent
Paid attention to punctuation

Needs Work 1 2 3 4 5 Excellent
Sounded good

Total Words Read _____

Total Errors − _____

Correct WPM _____

57

Fiction

from **"Brother Death"**

by Sherwood Anderson

	Words Read	Miscues

There was a back porch to the Grey house . . . and from the porch steps a path led down to a stone springhouse. A spring came out of the ground just there, and there was a tiny stream that went along the edge of a field, past two large barns and out across a meadow to a creek—called a "branch" in Virginia, and the two trees stood close together beyond the springhouse and the fence.

They were [strong] trees, their roots down in the rich, always damp soil, and one of them had a great limb that came down near the ground, so that Ted and Mary could climb into it and out another limb into its brother tree, and in the fall, when other trees, at the front and side of the house, had shed their leaves, blood-red leaves still clung to the two oaks. They were like dry blood on gray days, but on other days, when the sun came out, the trees flamed against distant hills. The leaves clung, whispering and talking when the wind blew, so that the trees themselves seemed carrying on a conversation.

John Grey had decided he would have the trees cut. At first it was not a very definite decision. "I think I'll have them cut," he announced.

"But why?" his wife asked.

Words Read
12
24
37
51
63
73
75
86
99
112
125
138
150
163
173
184
189
202
215
216
221

Needs Work 1 2 3 4 5 Excellent
Paid attention to punctuation

Needs Work 1 2 3 4 5 Excellent
Sounded good

Total Words Read _____

Total Errors − _____

Correct WPM _____

58
Nonfiction

from *Into the Deep Forest with Henry David Thoreau*
by Jim Murphy

First Reading

	Words Read	Miscues

"I think that I cannot preserve my health and spirits," Henry — 11 — ____

David Thoreau wrote in his journal, "unless I spend four hours a — 23 — ____

day . . . sauntering through the woods and over the hills and — 33 — ____

fields, absolutely free from all worldly engagements." — 40 — ____

And so, every day for over thirty years, Henry would leave — 51 — ____

his home in Concord, Massachusetts, and stride through the — 60 — ____

surrounding swamps and brush and forest. It was only when he — 71 — ____

was away from town and the prying eyes of his neighbors that — 83 — ____

Henry felt truly free—to follow any path he chose, to study — 95 — ____

carefully what was around him, and to think any thought — 105 — ____

he wanted. — 107 — ____

Few people meeting Henry for the first time would take — 117 — ____

him for much of a thinker. He liked to wear simple work shirts, — 130 — ____

rumpled pants, and boots that were heavily greased to keep water — 141 — ____

out. What is more, his hands were rough from years of hard work, — 154 — ____

while constant exposure to sun, rain, and icy winds had left his — 166 — ____

face tanned and deeply lined. But if his appearance was — 176 — ____

unremarkable, his mind was not. In fact, Henry David Thoreau is — 187 — ____

now considered one of the great American writers, philosophers, — 196 — ____

and naturalists of the nineteenth century. — 202 — ____

Needs Work   1 2 3 4 5   Excellent
Paid attention to punctuation

Needs Work   1 2 3 4 5   Excellent
Sounded good

Total Words Read _____

Total Errors – _____

Correct WPM _____

58

Nonfiction

from *Into the Deep Forest with Henry David Thoreau*

by Jim Murphy

Second Reading

	Words Read	Miscues

"I think that I cannot preserve my health and spirits," Henry — 11

David Thoreau wrote in his journal, "unless I spend four hours a — 23

day . . . sauntering through the woods and over the hills and — 33

fields, absolutely free from all worldly engagements." — 40

And so, every day for over thirty years, Henry would leave — 51

his home in Concord, Massachusetts, and stride through the — 60

surrounding swamps and brush and forest. It was only when he — 71

was away from town and the prying eyes of his neighbors that — 83

Henry felt truly free—to follow any path he chose, to study — 95

carefully what was around him, and to think any thought — 105

he wanted. — 107

Few people meeting Henry for the first time would take — 117

him for much of a thinker. He liked to wear simple work shirts, — 130

rumpled pants, and boots that were heavily greased to keep water — 141

out. What is more, his hands were rough from years of hard work, — 154

while constant exposure to sun, rain, and icy winds had left his — 166

face tanned and deeply lined. But if his appearance was — 176

unremarkable, his mind was not. In fact, Henry David Thoreau is — 187

now considered one of the great American writers, philosophers, — 196

and naturalists of the nineteenth century. — 202

Needs Work   1   2   3   4   5   Excellent
Paid attention to punctuation

Needs Work   1   2   3   4   5   Excellent
Sounded good

Total Words Read _____

Total Errors − _____

Correct WPM _____

59

Nonfiction

from *On the Brink of Extinction:*
The California Condor
by Caroline Arnold

First Reading

	Words Read	Miscues

A group of scientists watched anxiously as AC-9, the last of the free-flying California condors, circled overhead. Gliding gracefully on giant wings, the huge bird eyed the fresh carcass that lay in the clearing. Like other vultures, it depended on finding dead animals for its food. Finally AC-9 landed and cautiously approached the meat. Before the bird had time to escape, the scientists released their net and caught it. One person rushed forward to grab the condor and safely untangle it while another brought over a small carrier in which they would transport the bird to the zoo. AC-9 and the twenty-six other condors already in captivity were the only California condors left in the world. If they died, their species would become extinct. The scientists hoped that placing these birds together in male-female pairs would lead to successful breeding in zoos. After a few years, young condors could be returned to the wild to begin a new healthy flock.

For forty thousand years or more, California condors ranged across much of North America. They fed on the carcasses of giant sloths, mastodons, and other large mammals that roamed the continent during the last Ice Age. When these animals became extinct about ten thousand years ago, the condors disappeared everywhere except along the west coast.

Words Read
12
19
33
43
53
64
76
87
99
109
120
129
139
150
160
169
181
190
200
209
215

Needs Work   1   2   3   4   5   Excellent
Paid attention to punctuation

Needs Work   1   2   3   4   5   Excellent
Sounded good

Total Words Read _____

Total Errors – _____

Correct WPM _____

117

59

Nonfiction

from *On the Brink of Extinction:*
The California Condor
by Caroline Arnold

	Words Read	Miscues

A group of scientists watched anxiously as AC-9, the last of the | 12 | ——— |
free-flying California condors, circled overhead. Gliding gracefully | 19 | ——— |
on giant wings, the huge bird eyed the fresh carcass that lay in the | 33 | ——— |
clearing. Like other vultures, it depended on finding dead animals | 43 | ——— |
for its food. Finally AC-9 landed and cautiously approached the | 53 | ——— |
meat. Before the bird had time to escape, the scientists released | 64 | ——— |
their net and caught it. One person rushed forward to grab the | 76 | ——— |
condor and safely untangle it while another brought over a small | 87 | ——— |
carrier in which they would transport the bird to the zoo. AC-9 | 99 | ——— |
and the twenty-six other condors already in captivity were the | 109 | ——— |
only California condors left in the world. If they died, their | 120 | ——— |
species would become extinct. The scientists hoped that placing | 129 | ——— |
these birds together in male-female pairs would lead to successful | 139 | ——— |
breeding in zoos. After a few years, young condors could be | 150 | ——— |
returned to the wild to begin a new healthy flock. | 160 | ——— |

For forty thousand years or more, California condors ranged | 169 | ——— |
across much of North America. They fed on the carcasses of giant | 181 | ——— |
sloths, mastodons, and other large mammals that roamed the | 190 | ——— |
continent during the last Ice Age. When these animals became | 200 | ——— |
extinct about ten thousand years ago, the condors disappeared | 209 | ——— |
everywhere except along the west coast. | 215 | ——— |

Needs Work   1   2   3   4   5   Excellent
Paid attention to punctuation

Needs Work   1   2   3   4   5   Excellent
Sounded good

Total Words Read ————————

Total Errors – ————————

Correct WPM ————————

60

Fiction

from *My Daniel*
by Pam Conrad

	Words Read	Miscues

I thought it was fun in those days to see Pa strapped to a plow — 15 — _____

like a horse, a workhorse that plodded along wordlessly while — 25 — _____

Ma steered the plow through the hard soil. I was too little to — 38 — _____

understand how poor we were. — 43 — _____

    I remember how everything was so slow and thick—the air, — 54 — _____

the sky, the dirt; Daniel's job was to plant the seeds. I followed — 67 — _____

along beside him through the heavy clods of dirt and watched as — 79 — _____

he dropped one seed after another before each of his bare feet. — 91 — _____

Daniel carried a sack full of seeds on his shoulder, and it seems I — 105 — _____

can remember him pulling a dry twig or flower out of the sack — 118 — _____

and tossing it at me with a big grin. The grin. I search my — 132 — _____

memories for the exact slant of his smile. — 140 — _____

    And then suddenly Daniel dropped to his knees in the soil. I — 152 — _____

crouched next to him, my hand on his knee, and watched as he — 165 — _____

pulled rocks from the dirt. The rocks were the size of the palm of — 179 — _____

my hand, and there—hundreds and hundreds of miles from any — 190 — _____

seashore—he had licked his fingers and, darkening the surfaces — 200 — _____

of the rocks, brought life to the delicate designs of clams and — 212 — _____

tiny seashells. — 214 — _____

    "Look, Julie," he had said, holding it out to me. — 224 — _____

Needs Work   1   2   3   4   5   Excellent
Paid attention to punctuation

Needs Work   1   2   3   4   5   Excellent
Sounded good

Total Words Read   _____

Total Errors − _____

Correct WPM   _____

from *My Daniel*

by Pam Conrad

	Words Read	Miscues
I thought it was fun in those days to see Pa strapped to a plow	15	_____
like a horse, a workhorse that plodded along wordlessly while	25	_____
Ma steered the plow through the hard soil. I was too little to	38	_____
understand how poor we were.	43	_____
I remember how everything was so slow and thick—the air,	54	_____
the sky, the dirt; Daniel's job was to plant the seeds. I followed	67	_____
along beside him through the heavy clods of dirt and watched as	79	_____
he dropped one seed after another before each of his bare feet.	91	_____
Daniel carried a sack full of seeds on his shoulder, and it seems I	105	_____
can remember him pulling a dry twig or flower out of the sack	118	_____
and tossing it at me with a big grin. The grin. I search my	132	_____
memories for the exact slant of his smile.	140	_____
And then suddenly Daniel dropped to his knees in the soil. I	152	_____
crouched next to him, my hand on his knee, and watched as he	165	_____
pulled rocks from the dirt. The rocks were the size of the palm of	179	_____
my hand, and there—hundreds and hundreds of miles from any	190	_____
seashore—he had licked his fingers and, darkening the surfaces	200	_____
of the rocks, brought life to the delicate designs of clams and	212	_____
tiny seashells.	214	_____
"Look, Julie," he had said, holding it out to me.	224	_____

Needs Work   1   2   3   4   5   Excellent
Paid attention to punctuation

Needs Work   1   2   3   4   5   Excellent
Sounded good

Total Words Read   _____

Total Errors   −_____

Correct WPM   _____

61

Fiction

from *Survival: Earthquake*
by K. Duey and K. A. Bale

First Reading

	Words Read	Miscues

It was almost dawn. Brendan O'Connor gripped the reins,   9   _____

struggling to control the nervous mare without slowing her down.   19   _____

Up and down Market Street wagon wheels gritted over the   29   _____

cobblestones. Drivers were hauling produce, laundry, milk,   36   _____

everything the hotels and restaurants would need for the   45   _____

day's business.   47   _____

      Brendan had worked hard to get this route and he wasn't   58   _____

going to lose it. His boss had the kind of temper no one wanted   72   _____

to set off. Two things made old man Hansen furious: losing   83   _____

money and late deliveries. Fancy San Francisco hotels like the   93   _____

Baldwin and the Palace would find another bakery if their wealthy   104   _____

guests had to wait for their fresh-baked bread and pastries.   114   _____

      The street lamps had been turned off a few minutes before   125   _____

and the city was enveloped by a deep blue predawn glow.   136   _____

Brendan shivered. The damp early morning chill seeped through   145   _____

his worn woolen jacket. He looked up at the fading crescent   156   _____

moon. There wasn't a cloud in the sky. Maybe it would be warmer   169   _____

today. Still, he needed to find a better blanket for his cot soon.   182   _____

      So far, no one had objected to his sleeping in a corner of the   196   _____

furniture warehouse.   198   _____

Needs Work   1   2   3   4   5   Excellent
Paid attention to punctuation

Needs Work   1   2   3   4   5   Excellent
Sounded good

Total Words Read _____

Total Errors − _____

Correct WPM _____

from *Survival: Earthquake*
by K. Duey and K. A. Bale

	Words Read	Miscues

It was almost dawn. Brendan O'Connor gripped the reins, — 9 _____

struggling to control the nervous mare without slowing her down. — 19 _____

Up and down Market Street wagon wheels gritted over the — 29 _____

cobblestones. Drivers were hauling produce, laundry, milk, — 36 _____

everything the hotels and restaurants would need for the — 45 _____

day's business. — 47 _____

Brendan had worked hard to get this route and he wasn't — 58 _____

going to lose it. His boss had the kind of temper no one wanted — 72 _____

to set off. Two things made old man Hansen furious: losing — 83 _____

money and late deliveries. Fancy San Francisco hotels like the — 93 _____

Baldwin and the Palace would find another bakery if their wealthy — 104 _____

guests had to wait for their fresh-baked bread and pastries. — 114 _____

The street lamps had been turned off a few minutes before — 125 _____

and the city was enveloped by a deep blue predawn glow. — 136 _____

Brendan shivered. The damp early morning chill seeped through — 145 _____

his worn woolen jacket. He looked up at the fading crescent — 156 _____

moon. There wasn't a cloud in the sky. Maybe it would be warmer — 169 _____

today. Still, he needed to find a better blanket for his cot soon. — 182 _____

So far, no one had objected to his sleeping in a corner of the — 196 _____

furniture warehouse. — 198 _____

Needs Work 1 2 3 4 5 Excellent
Paid attention to punctuation

Needs Work 1 2 3 4 5 Excellent
Sounded good

Total Words Read _____

Total Errors − _____

Correct WPM _____

62

Nonfiction

from **"Pizza in Warsaw,
Torte in Prague"**

by Slavenka Drakulić

First Reading

	Words Read	Miscues

Right after the overthrow of the Ceausescu government in   9   _____
Romania in December 1989, I read a report in the newspaper   20   _____
about life in Bucharest. There was a story about a man who ate   33   _____
the first banana in his life. He was an older man, a worker, and he   48   _____
said to a reporter shyly that he ate a whole banana, together with   61   _____
the skin, because he didn't know that he had to peel it. At first, I   76   _____
was moved by the isolation this man was forced to live in, by the   90   _____
fact that he never read or even heard what to do with a banana.   104   _____
But then something else caught my attention: *"It tasted good,"* he   115   _____
said. I can imagine this man, holding a sweet-smelling, ripe   125   _____
banana in his hand, curious and excited by it, as by a forbidden   138   _____
fruit. He holds it for a moment, then bites. It tastes strange but   151   _____
"good." It must have been good, even together with a bitter, tough   163   _____
skin, because it was something unachievable, an object of desire.   173   _____
It was not a banana that he was eating, but the promise, the hope   187   _____
of the future. So, he liked it no matter what its taste.   199   _____

Needs Work   1   2   3   4   5   Excellent
Paid attention to punctuation

Needs Work   1   2   3   4   5   Excellent
Sounded good

Total Words Read _____

Total Errors − _____

Correct WPM _____

62
Nonfiction

from "Pizza in Warsaw, Torte in Prague"

by Slavenka Drakulić

Second Reading

	Words Read	Miscues

Right after the overthrow of the Ceausescu government in   9   _____

Romania in December 1989, I read a report in the newspaper   20   _____

about life in Bucharest. There was a story about a man who ate   33   _____

the first banana in his life. He was an older man, a worker, and he   48   _____

said to a reporter shyly that he ate a whole banana, together with   61   _____

the skin, because he didn't know that he had to peel it. At first, I   76   _____

was moved by the isolation this man was forced to live in, by the   90   _____

fact that he never read or even heard what to do with a banana.   104   _____

But then something else caught my attention: *"It tasted good,"* he   115   _____

said. I can imagine this man, holding a sweet-smelling, ripe   125   _____

banana in his hand, curious and excited by it, as by a forbidden   138   _____

fruit. He holds it for a moment, then bites. It tastes strange but   151   _____

"good." It must have been good, even together with a bitter, tough   163   _____

skin, because it was something unachievable, an object of desire.   173   _____

It was not a banana that he was eating, but the promise, the hope   187   _____

of the future. So, he liked it no matter what its taste.   199   _____

Needs Work   1   2   3   4   5   Excellent
Paid attention to punctuation

Needs Work   1   2   3   4   5   Excellent
Sounded good

Total Words Read   _____

Total Errors − _____

Correct WPM   _____

63
Fiction

from "President Cleveland, Where Are You?"

by Robert Cormier

	Words Read	Miscues
First Reading		

∘∘∘

That was the autumn of the cowboy cards—Buck Jones and	11
Tom Tyler and Hoot Gibson and especially Ken Maynard. The	21
cards were available in those five-cent packages of gum: pink	31
sticks, three together, covered with a sweet white powder. You	41
couldn't blow bubbles with that particular gum, but it couldn't	51
have mattered less. The cowboy cards were important—the	60
pictures of those rock-faced men with eyes of blue steel.	70
On those wind-swept, leaf-tumbling afternoons we gathered	77
after school on the sidewalk in front of Lemire's Drugstore, across	88
from St. Jude's Parochial School, and we swapped and bargained	98
and matched for the cards. Because a Ken Maynard serial was	109
playing at the Globe every Saturday afternoon, he was the most	120
popular cowboy of all, and one of his cards was worth at least ten	134
of any other kind. Rollie Tremaine had a treasure of thirty or so,	147
and he guarded them jealously. He'd match you for the other	158
cards, but he risked his Ken Maynards only when the other kids	170
threatened to leave him out of the competition altogether.	179
You could almost hate Rollie Tremaine. In the first place, he	190
was the only son of Auguste Tremaine, who operated the Uptown	201
Dry Goods Store, and he did not live in a tenement.	212

Needs Work   1 2 3 4 5   Excellent
Paid attention to punctuation

Needs Work   1 2 3 4 5   Excellent
Sounded good

Total Words Read _____

Total Errors − _____

Correct WPM _____

63

Fiction

from "President Cleveland, Where Are You?"

by Robert Cormier

	Words Read	Miscues

That was the autumn of the cowboy cards—Buck Jones and   11 _____
Tom Tyler and Hoot Gibson and especially Ken Maynard. The   21 _____
cards were available in those five-cent packages of gum: pink   31 _____
sticks, three together, covered with a sweet white powder. You   41 _____
couldn't blow bubbles with that particular gum, but it couldn't   51 _____
have mattered less. The cowboy cards were important—the   60 _____
pictures of those rock-faced men with eyes of blue steel.   70 _____

On those wind-swept, leaf-tumbling afternoons we gathered   77 _____
after school on the sidewalk in front of Lemire's Drugstore, across   88 _____
from St. Jude's Parochial School, and we swapped and bargained   98 _____
and matched for the cards. Because a Ken Maynard serial was   109 _____
playing at the Globe every Saturday afternoon, he was the most   120 _____
popular cowboy of all, and one of his cards was worth at least ten   134 _____
of any other kind. Rollie Tremaine had a treasure of thirty or so,   147 _____
and he guarded them jealously. He'd match you for the other   158 _____
cards, but he risked his Ken Maynards only when the other kids   170 _____
threatened to leave him out of the competition altogether.   179 _____

You could almost hate Rollie Tremaine. In the first place, he   190 _____
was the only son of Auguste Tremaine, who operated the Uptown   201 _____
Dry Goods Store, and he did not live in a tenement.   212 _____

Needs Work   1 2 3 4 5   Excellent
Paid attention to punctuation

Needs Work   1 2 3 4 5   Excellent
Sounded good

Total Words Read _____

Total Errors − _____

Correct WPM _____

from *Horns of Plenty*
by Jane and Paul Annixter

Fiction

64

	Words Read	Miscues

The eagle screamed and the ram felt the impact of the human | 12 | _____
gaze, and threat again. The man did not reach for the gun; even | 25 | _____
if he had [the ram] Big Eye knew instinctively that the distance | 37 | _____
between was too great for danger. So he held his ground and | 49 | _____
crossed gazes with the man as if in challenge, while his hyper- | 61 | _____
awareness, born of his leadership, expanded and grew. | 69 | _____

For the old ram each rising of the sun, each change of weather | 82 | _____
or shift of wind called for new strategy. Each day brought fresh | 94 | _____
problems to be solved. These he must always sense in advance, for | 106 | _____
with his band his authority was absolute, based as it was upon | 118 | _____
the primal law of the strongest, wisest and most courageous. His | 129 | _____
was a total responsibility, for where he led the band would follow. | 141 | _____
If he chose to go down the sheer face of a precipice where the | 155 | _____
only way was a series of leaps and balancings from one nubbin of | 168 | _____
rock to another and thence to an almost non-existent ledge, the | 179 | _____
flock would unhesitatingly follow. If in crises he were to leap to | 191 | _____
his death in some sheer abyss, there, too, the flock would go. | 203 | _____

Needs Work   1 2 3 4 5   Excellent
Paid attention to punctuation

Needs Work   1 2 3 4 5   Excellent
Sounded good

Total Words Read _____

Total Errors − _____

Correct WPM _____

from *Horns of Plenty*

by Jane and Paul Annixter

	Words Read	Miscues
The eagle screamed and the ram felt the impact of the human	12	_____
gaze, and threat again. The man did not reach for the gun; even	25	_____
if he had [the ram] Big Eye knew instinctively that the distance	37	_____
between was too great for danger. So he held his ground and	49	_____
crossed gazes with the man as if in challenge, while his hyper-	61	_____
awareness, born of his leadership, expanded and grew.	69	_____
For the old ram each rising of the sun, each change of weather	82	_____
or shift of wind called for new strategy. Each day brought fresh	94	_____
problems to be solved. These he must always sense in advance, for	106	_____
with his band his authority was absolute, based as it was upon	118	_____
the primal law of the strongest, wisest and most courageous. His	129	_____
was a total responsibility, for where he led the band would follow.	141	_____
If he chose to go down the sheer face of a precipice where the	155	_____
only way was a series of leaps and balancings from one nubbin of	168	_____
rock to another and thence to an almost non-existent ledge, the	179	_____
flock would unhesitatingly follow. If in crises he were to leap to	191	_____
his death in some sheer abyss, there, too, the flock would go.	203	_____

Needs Work   1   2   3   4   5   Excellent
Paid attention to punctuation

Needs Work   1   2   3   4   5   Excellent
Sounded good

Total Words Read   _____

Total Errors   − _____

Correct WPM   _____

65 Fiction

from *The Lost Dispatch:*
A Story of Antietam
by Donald J. Sobol

First Reading

	Words Read	Miscues

A mile raced by, and then another. With every passing second — 11 ——

Wade expected to hear the shrill whine of a bullet reaching for — 23 ——

him. Farther and farther from the Union camps he sped, body — 34 ——

cramped low and cheek laid by [his horse] Outcast's plunging — 44 ——

neck. But no rifle blast pierced the clenching stillness, no bullet — 55 ——

singled him out. Night rested softly upon a land seemingly asleep — 66 ——

and harmless. — 68 ——

At length he shifted up into the saddle and stole a rearward — 80 ——

glance. The road behind lay straight for several hundred yards, — 90 ——

and empty. He slowed Outcast to a trot, musing indignantly. . . . — 100 ——

Mysterious sharpshooter—in a pig's ear! — 106 ——

Believing himself absolutely safe, he remained seated upright — 114 ——

in the saddle. After crossing the James River on an old flatboat, he — 127 ——

headed due west for Kentucky. A spring rain began to fall, and he — 140 ——

dismounted to unstrap the slicker. — 145 ——

As his weight dropped upon one foot, the realization of why — 156 ——

he had ridden this far unscathed darted through his mind. — 166 ——

A skilled marksman makes sure of his first shot, or does not — 178 ——

shoot. Darkness and now rain made a galloping target too difficult — 189 ——

to bring down. Far from being a daydream, Three-Fingers might — 199 ——

well be all too real—a marksman who was biding his time and — 212 ——

picking his spot. — 215 ——

Needs Work   1 2 3 4 5   Excellent
Paid attention to punctuation

Needs Work   1 2 3 4 5   Excellent
Sounded good

Total Words Read   _____

Total Errors − _____

Correct WPM   _____

65

Fiction

from *The Lost Dispatch:*

A Story of Antietam

by Donald J. Sobol

	Second Reading	
	Words Read	**Miscues**

	Words Read	Miscues

A mile raced by, and then another. With every passing second   11   _____

Wade expected to hear the shrill whine of a bullet reaching for   23   _____

him. Farther and farther from the Union camps he sped, body   34   _____

cramped low and cheek laid by [his horse] Outcast's plunging   44   _____

neck. But no rifle blast pierced the clenching stillness, no bullet   55   _____

singled him out. Night rested softly upon a land seemingly asleep   66   _____

and harmless.   68   _____

At length he shifted up into the saddle and stole a rearward   80   _____

glance. The road behind lay straight for several hundred yards,   90   _____

and empty. He slowed Outcast to a trot, musing indignantly. . . .   100   _____

Mysterious sharpshooter—in a pig's ear!   106   _____

Believing himself absolutely safe, he remained seated upright   114   _____

in the saddle. After crossing the James River on an old flatboat, he   127   _____

headed due west for Kentucky. A spring rain began to fall, and he   140   _____

dismounted to unstrap the slicker.   145   _____

As his weight dropped upon one foot, the realization of why   156   _____

he had ridden this far unscathed darted through his mind.   166   _____

A skilled marksman makes sure of his first shot, or does not   178   _____

shoot. Darkness and now rain made a galloping target too difficult   189   _____

to bring down. Far from being a daydream, Three-Fingers might   199   _____

well be all too real—a marksman who was biding his time and   212   _____

picking his spot.   215   _____

Needs Work   1 2 3 4 5   Excellent

Paid attention to punctuation

Needs Work   1 2 3 4 5   Excellent

Sounded good

Total Words Read   _____

Total Errors – _____

Correct WPM   _____

66 Nonfiction
from *Adventures in Courage*
by Dennis Brennan

	Words Read	Miscues

The development of the dirigible marked the final phase of the | 11 | _____

history of the balloon. These gigantic airships became a popular | 21 | _____

means of air transportation. They could carry passengers great | 30 | _____

distances, even across oceans. | 34 | _____

On May 3, 1937, a tragic accident climaxed the story of the | 46 | _____

dirigible. On that day a giant airship named the *Hindenburg* | 56 | _____

exploded while landing at Lakehurst, New Jersey, at the end of a | 68 | _____

transoceanic trip from Germany. Thirty-six of the 97 passengers | 77 | _____

aboard were killed and many more were horribly burned. This | 87 | _____

tragedy brought the era of the balloon to its end. Although | 98 | _____

dirigibles still are occasionally seen in the skies, their use has | 109 | _____

become very limited. | 112 | _____

But even during the nineteenth century, many believed the | 121 | _____

balloon was not the final answer to man's desire for equality with | 133 | _____

the birds. They believed the true future of aviation lay in flight | 145 | _____

with winged aircraft, not with bulky, gas-filled bags. | 153 | _____

Balloons flew because the gas inside them was lighter than the | 164 | _____

air. But birds are heavier than air, reasoned the men of the sky, | 177 | _____

and *they* fly. | 180 | _____

How? | 181 | _____

That was the question. How? | 186 | _____

Is it not possible, they asked themselves, for man to construct | 197 | _____

a machine that would duplicate birds' flight? | 204 | _____

Yes, they answered. It *is* possible. | 210 | _____

Needs Work   1   2   3   4   5   Excellent
Paid attention to punctuation

Needs Work   1   2   3   4   5   Excellent
Sounded good

Total Words Read _____

Total Errors − _____

Correct WPM _____

from *Adventures in Courage*
by Dennis Brennan

The development of the dirigible marked the final phase of the | 11 | _____

history of the balloon. These gigantic airships became a popular | 21 | _____

means of air transportation. They could carry passengers great | 30 | _____

distances, even across oceans. | 34 | _____

On May 3, 1937, a tragic accident climaxed the story of the | 46 | _____

dirigible. On that day a giant airship named the *Hindenburg* | 56 | _____

exploded while landing at Lakehurst, New Jersey, at the end of a | 68 | _____

transoceanic trip from Germany. Thirty-six of the 97 passengers | 77 | _____

aboard were killed and many more were horribly burned. This | 87 | _____

tragedy brought the era of the balloon to its end. Although | 98 | _____

dirigibles still are occasionally seen in the skies, their use has | 109 | _____

become very limited. | 112 | _____

But even during the nineteenth century, many believed the | 121 | _____

balloon was not the final answer to man's desire for equality with | 133 | _____

the birds. They believed the true future of aviation lay in flight | 145 | _____

with winged aircraft, not with bulky, gas-filled bags. | 153 | _____

Balloons flew because the gas inside them was lighter than the | 164 | _____

air. But birds are heavier than air, reasoned the men of the sky, | 177 | _____

and *they* fly. | 180 | _____

How? | 181 | _____

That was the question. How? | 186 | _____

Is it not possible, they asked themselves, for man to construct | 197 | _____

a machine that would duplicate birds' flight? | 204 | _____

Yes, they answered. It *is* possible. | 210 | _____

Needs Work   1   2   3   4   5   Excellent
          Paid attention to punctuation

Needs Work   1   2   3   4   5   Excellent
          Sounded good

Total Words Read   _____

Total Errors   −_____

Correct WPM   _____

67

Fiction

from **"Sweet Potato Pie"**

by Eugenia Collier

First Reading

	Words Read	Miscues

From up here on the fourteenth floor, my brother Charley
looks like an insect scurrying among other insects. A deep feeling
of love surges through me. Despite the distance, he seems to feel
it, for he turns and scans the upper windows, but failing to find
me, continues on his way.

I watch him moving quickly—gingerly, it seems to me—down
Fifth Avenue and around the corner to his shabby taxicab. In a
moment he will be heading back uptown.

I turn from the window and flop down on the bed, shoes and
all. Perhaps because of what happened this afternoon or maybe
just because I see Charley so seldom, my thoughts hover over him
like hummingbirds. The cheerful, impersonal tidiness of this room
is a world away from Charley's walk-up flat in Harlem and a
hundred worlds from the bare, noisy shanty where he and the rest
of us spent what there was of childhood. I close my eyes, and side
by side I see the Charley of my boyhood and the Charley of this
afternoon, as clearly as if I were looking at a split TV screen.
Another surge of love, seasoned with gratitude, wells up in me.

Words Read
10 _____
21 _____
33 _____
46 _____
51 _____
62 _____
74 _____
81 _____
94 _____
104 _____
116 _____
125 _____
137 _____
149 _____
163 _____
177 _____
190 _____
201 _____

Needs Work   1 2 3 4 5   Excellent
Paid attention to punctuation

Needs Work   1 2 3 4 5   Excellent
Sounded good

Total Words Read _____

Total Errors − _____

Correct WPM _____

67

Fiction

from **"Sweet Potato Pie"**

by Eugenia Collier

	Words Read	Miscues

From up here on the fourteenth floor, my brother Charley   10 _____

looks like an insect scurrying among other insects. A deep feeling   21 _____

of love surges through me. Despite the distance, he seems to feel   33 _____

it, for he turns and scans the upper windows, but failing to find   46 _____

me, continues on his way.   51 _____

    I watch him moving quickly—gingerly, it seems to me—down   62 _____

Fifth Avenue and around the corner to his shabby taxicab. In a   74 _____

moment he will be heading back uptown.   81 _____

    I turn from the window and flop down on the bed, shoes and   94 _____

all. Perhaps because of what happened this afternoon or maybe   104 _____

just because I see Charley so seldom, my thoughts hover over him   116 _____

like hummingbirds. The cheerful, impersonal tidiness of this room   125 _____

is a world away from Charley's walk-up flat in Harlem and a   137 _____

hundred worlds from the bare, noisy shanty where he and the rest   149 _____

of us spent what there was of childhood. I close my eyes, and side   163 _____

by side I see the Charley of my boyhood and the Charley of this   177 _____

afternoon, as clearly as if I were looking at a split TV screen.   190 _____

Another surge of love, seasoned with gratitude, wells up in me.   201 _____

Needs Work   1   2   3   4   5   Excellent
Paid attention to punctuation

Needs Work   1   2   3   4   5   Excellent
Sounded good

Total Words Read _____

Total Errors – _____

Correct WPM _____

68

Fiction

from "A Walk to the Jetty"
by Jamaica Kincaid

First Reading

	Words Read	Miscues

When my father's stomach started to go bad, the doctor had   11 _____

recommended a walk every evening right after he ate his dinner.   22 _____

Sometimes he would take me with him. When he took me with   34 _____

him, we usually went to the jetty, and there he would sit and talk   48 _____

to the night watchman about cricket or some other thing that   59 _____

didn't interest me, because it was not personal; they didn't talk   70 _____

about their wives, or their children, or their parents, or about any   82 _____

of their likes and dislikes. They talked about things in such a   94 _____

strange way, and I didn't see what they found funny, but   105 _____

sometimes they made each other laugh so much that their guffaws   116 _____

would bound out to sea and send back an echo. I was always   129 _____

sorry when we got to the jetty and saw that the night watchman   142 _____

on duty was the one he enjoyed speaking to; it was like being   155 _____

locked up in a book filled with numbers and diagrams and what-   167 _____

ifs. For the thing about not being able to understand and enjoy   178 _____

what they were saying was I had nothing to take my mind off my   192 _____

fear of slipping in between the boards of the jetty.   202 _____

Needs Work   1 2 3 4 5   Excellent
Paid attention to punctuation

Needs Work   1 2 3 4 5   Excellent
Sounded good

Total Words Read _____

Total Errors − _____

Correct WPM _____

from "A Walk to the Jetty"
by Jamaica Kincaid

	Words Read	Miscues

When my father's stomach started to go bad, the doctor had   11   _____

recommended a walk every evening right after he ate his dinner.   22   _____

Sometimes he would take me with him. When he took me with   34   _____

him, we usually went to the jetty, and there he would sit and talk   48   _____

to the night watchman about cricket or some other thing that   59   _____

didn't interest me, because it was not personal; they didn't talk   70   _____

about their wives, or their children, or their parents, or about any 82   _____

of their likes and dislikes. They talked about things in such a   94   _____

strange way, and I didn't see what they found funny, but   105   _____

sometimes they made each other laugh so much that their guffaws   116   _____

would bound out to sea and send back an echo. I was always   129   _____

sorry when we got to the jetty and saw that the night watchman   142   _____

on duty was the one he enjoyed speaking to; it was like being   155   _____

locked up in a book filled with numbers and diagrams and what-   167   _____

ifs. For the thing about not being able to understand and enjoy   178   _____

what they were saying was I had nothing to take my mind off my   192   _____

fear of slipping in between the boards of the jetty.   202   _____

Needs Work   1 2 3 4 5   Excellent
Paid attention to punctuation

Needs Work   1 2 3 4 5   Excellent
Sounded good

Total Words Read   _____

Total Errors − _____

Correct WPM   _____

69

Nonfiction

from *My Year*
by Roald Dahl

	Words Read	Miscues

No cuckoo has ever bothered to build its own nest or hatch or — 13 _____

feed its young. The female (carrying her egg in her beak) searches — 25 _____

the hedgerows until she finds the nest of another bird that — 36 _____

already has eggs in it, and she slips her own egg in with the others — 51 _____

and flies away and forgets all about it. — 59 _____

    Usually, for some unknown reason, cuckoos choose a hedge — 68 _____

sparrow's nest. . . . The extraordinary thing is that the mother — 77 _____

hedge sparrow, when she returns and finds this dirty brown egg — 88 _____

lying in her nest among her own blue beauties, does not seem to — 101 _____

mind at all and proceeds to sit on it and incubate it together with — 115 _____

her own. — 117 _____

    Little does she know what is going to happen when all the — 129 _____

eggs hatch. There will usually be four or five of her own eggs plus — 143 _____

the one cuckoo's egg and when the baby chicks hatch out, the — 155 _____

mother and father both feed them all, including the horrid cuckoo — 166 _____

chick. Don't forget that the adult cuckoo is a bird three times as — 179 _____

big as the hedge sparrow, and therefore the cuckoo chick grows — 190 _____

three times as fast as the little sparrows. Then comes the — 201 _____

slaughter. The overgrown baby cuckoo proceeds quite literally to — 210 _____

push the baby hedge sparrows one by one out of the nest to die. — 224 _____

Needs Work   1   2   3   4   5   Excellent
Paid attention to punctuation

Needs Work   1   2   3   4   5   Excellent
Sounded good

Total Words Read _____

Total Errors — _____

Correct WPM _____

from *My Year*
by Roald Dahl

No cuckoo has ever bothered to build its own nest or hatch or   **13** _____

feed its young. The female (carrying her egg in her beak) searches   **25** _____

the hedgerows until she finds the nest of another bird that   **36** _____

already has eggs in it, and she slips her own egg in with the others   **51** _____

and flies away and forgets all about it.   **59** _____

    Usually, for some unknown reason, cuckoos choose a hedge   **68** _____

sparrow's nest. . . . The extraordinary thing is that the mother   **77** _____

hedge sparrow, when she returns and finds this dirty brown egg   **88** _____

lying in her nest among her own blue beauties, does not seem to   **101** _____

mind at all and proceeds to sit on it and incubate it together with   **115** _____

her own.   **117** _____

    Little does she know what is going to happen when all the   **129** _____

eggs hatch. There will usually be four or five of her own eggs plus   **143** _____

the one cuckoo's egg and when the baby chicks hatch out, the   **155** _____

mother and father both feed them all, including the horrid cuckoo   **166** _____

chick. Don't forget that the adult cuckoo is a bird three times as   **179** _____

big as the hedge sparrow, and therefore the cuckoo chick grows   **190** _____

three times as fast as the little sparrows. Then comes the   **201** _____

slaughter. The overgrown baby cuckoo proceeds quite literally to   **210** _____

push the baby hedge sparrows one by one out of the nest to die.   **224** _____

Needs Work 1 2 3 4 5 Excellent
      Paid attention to punctuation

Needs Work 1 2 3 4 5 Excellent
      Sounded good

Total Words Read _____

Total Errors – _____

Correct WPM _____

70

Nonfiction

from *The Road from Coorain*
by Jill Ker Conway

First Reading

	Words Read	Miscues

➣➣

Before being formally enrolled, I was taken for an interview   10 _____

with Miss Everett, the headmistress. To me she seemed like a   21 _____

benevolent being from another planet. She was over six feet tall,   32 _____

with the carriage and gait of a splendid athlete. Her dress was   44 _____

new to me. She wore a tweed suit of soft colors and battered   57 _____

elegance. She spoke in the plummy tones of a woman educated in   69 _____

England, and her intelligent face beamed with humor and   78 _____

curiosity. When she spoke, the habit of long years of teaching   89 _____

French made her articulate her words clearly and so forcefully   99 _____

that the unwary who stood too close were in danger of being   111 _____

sprayed like the audience too close to the footlights of a   122 _____

vaudeville show. "She looks strapping," she cheerfully commented   130 _____

to my mother, after talking to me for a few minutes alone. "She   143 _____

can begin tomorrow." Thereafter, no matter how I misbehaved, or   153 _____

what events brought me into her presence, I felt real benevolence   164 _____

radiating from Miss Everett.   168 _____

The sight of her upright figure, forever striding across the   178 _____

school grounds, automatically caused her charges to straighten   186 _____

their backs. Those who slouched were often startled to have her   197 _____

appear suddenly behind them and seize their shoulders to correct   207 _____

their posture.   209 _____

Needs Work   1   2   3   4   5   Excellent
Paid attention to punctuation

Needs Work   1   2   3   4   5   Excellent
Sounded good

Total Words Read _____

Total Errors − _____

Correct WPM _____

from *The Road from Coorain*

by Jill Ker Conway

	Words Read	Miscues
Before being formally enrolled, I was taken for an interview	10	_____
with Miss Everett, the headmistress. To me she seemed like a	21	_____
benevolent being from another planet. She was over six feet tall,	32	_____
with the carriage and gait of a splendid athlete. Her dress was	44	_____
new to me. She wore a tweed suit of soft colors and battered	57	_____
elegance. She spoke in the plummy tones of a woman educated in	69	_____
England, and her intelligent face beamed with humor and	78	_____
curiosity. When she spoke, the habit of long years of teaching	89	_____
French made her articulate her words clearly and so forcefully	99	_____
that the unwary who stood too close were in danger of being	111	_____
sprayed like the audience too close to the footlights of a	122	_____
vaudeville show. "She looks strapping," she cheerfully commented	130	_____
to my mother, after talking to me for a few minutes alone. "She	143	_____
can begin tomorrow." Thereafter, no matter how I misbehaved, or	153	_____
what events brought me into her presence, I felt real benevolence	164	_____
radiating from Miss Everett.	168	_____
The sight of her upright figure, forever striding across the	178	_____
school grounds, automatically caused her charges to straighten	186	_____
their backs. Those who slouched were often startled to have her	197	_____
appear suddenly behind them and seize their shoulders to correct	207	_____
their posture.	209	_____

Needs Work   1   2   3   4   5   Excellent
Paid attention to punctuation

Needs Work   1   2   3   4   5   Excellent
Sounded good

Total Words Read _____

Total Errors − _____

Correct WPM _____

71

Fiction

from *The Incredible Journey*
by Sheila Burnford

First Reading

	Words Read	Miscues

The late afternoon sun slanted through the branches overhead, — 9 _____

and it looked invitingly snug and secure. The old dog stood for a — 22 _____

minute, his heavy head hanging, and his tired body swaying — 32 _____

slightly, then lay down on his side in the hollow. The cat, after a — 46 _____

good deal of wary observation, made a little hollow among the — 57 _____

spruce needles and curled around in it, purring softly. The young — 68 _____

dog disappeared into the undergrowth and reappeared presently, — 76 _____

his smooth coat dripping water, to lie down a little away apart — 88 _____

from the others. — 91 _____

The old dog continued to pant exhaustedly for a long time, — 102 _____

one hind leg shaking badly, until his eyes closed at last, the — 114 _____

labored breaths came further and further apart, and he was — 124 _____

sleeping—still, save for an occasional long shudder. — 132 _____

Later on, when darkness fell, the young dog moved over and — 143 _____

stretched out closely at his side and the cat stalked over to lie — 156 _____

between his paws; and so, warmed and comforted by their — 166 _____

closeness, the old dog slept, momentarily unconscious of his — 175 _____

aching, tired body or his hunger. — 181 _____

In the nearby hills a timber wolf howled mournfully; owls — 191 _____

called and answered and glided silently by with great outspread — 201 _____

wings; and there were faint whispers of movement and small — 211 _____

rustling noises around all through the night. — 218 _____

Needs Work   1   2   3   4   5   Excellent
Paid attention to punctuation

Needs Work   1   2   3   4   5   Excellent
Sounded good

Total Words Read _____

Total Errors − _____

Correct WPM _____

141

from *The Incredible Journey*
by Sheila Burnford

The late afternoon sun slanted through the branches overhead,	9	_____
and it looked invitingly snug and secure. The old dog stood for a	22	_____
minute, his heavy head hanging, and his tired body swaying	32	_____
slightly, then lay down on his side in the hollow. The cat, after a	46	_____
good deal of wary observation, made a little hollow among the	57	_____
spruce needles and curled around in it, purring softly. The young	68	_____
dog disappeared into the undergrowth and reappeared presently,	76	_____
his smooth coat dripping water, to lie down a little away apart	88	_____
from the others.	91	_____
The old dog continued to pant exhaustedly for a long time,	102	_____
one hind leg shaking badly, until his eyes closed at last, the	114	_____
labored breaths came further and further apart, and he was	124	_____
sleeping—still, save for an occasional long shudder.	132	_____
Later on, when darkness fell, the young dog moved over and	143	_____
stretched out closely at his side and the cat stalked over to lie	156	_____
between his paws; and so, warmed and comforted by their	166	_____
closeness, the old dog slept, momentarily unconscious of his	175	_____
aching, tired body or his hunger.	181	_____
In the nearby hills a timber wolf howled mournfully; owls	191	_____
called and answered and glided silently by with great outspread	201	_____
wings; and there were faint whispers of movement and small	211	_____
rustling noises around all through the night.	218	_____

Needs Work   1   2   3   4   5   Excellent
    Paid attention to punctuation

Needs Work   1   2   3   4   5   Excellent
    Sounded good

Total Words Read _____

Total Errors − _____

Correct WPM _____

from *My Own Two Feet*
by Beverly Cleary

72

Nonfiction

First Reading

	Words Read	Miscues

The three of us, Mother, Dad, and I, stood on the sidewalk — 12 _____

outside the Greyhound bus station in Portland, Oregon, searching — 21 _____

for words we could not find or holding back words we could not — 34 _____

speak. The sun, bronze from the smoke of September forest fires, — 45 _____

cast an illusory light. Nothing seemed real, but it was. I was — 57 _____

leaving, actually leaving, for California, the Golden State, land of — 67 _____

poppies, big red geraniums, trees heavy with oranges, palm trees — 77 _____

beneath cloudless skies, and best of all, no Depression. I had seen — 89 _____

it all on postcards and in the movies, and so had the rest of my — 104 _____

class at Grant High School. California was the goal of many. John — 116 _____

Steinbeck had not yet, in 1934, revised our thinking. — 125 _____

And now I was one of the lucky ones going to this glorious — 138 _____

place where people made movies all day and danced the night — 149 _____

away. I was escaping the clatter of typewriters in business school — 160 _____

and going instead to college. As I stood there in the smoky light — 173 _____

in my neat navy blue dress, which Mother had measured a — 184 _____

fashionable twelve inches from the floor when I made it, and with — 196 _____

a five-dollar bill given to me by my father for emergencies rolled — 208 _____

in my stocking, I tried to hide my elation from my parents. — 220 _____

Needs Work   1 2 3 4 5   Excellent
Paid attention to punctuation

Needs Work   1 2 3 4 5   Excellent
Sounded good

Total Words Read   _____

Total Errors − _____

Correct WPM   _____

72

Nonfiction

from *My Own Two Feet*

by Beverly Cleary

The three of us, Mother, Dad, and I, stood on the sidewalk	12 _____
outside the Greyhound bus station in Portland, Oregon, searching	21 _____
for words we could not find or holding back words we could not	34 _____
speak. The sun, bronze from the smoke of September forest fires,	45 _____
cast an illusory light. Nothing seemed real, but it was. I was	57 _____
leaving, actually leaving, for California, the Golden State, land of	67 _____
poppies, big red geraniums, trees heavy with oranges, palm trees	77 _____
beneath cloudless skies, and best of all, no Depression. I had seen	89 _____
it all on postcards and in the movies, and so had the rest of my	104 _____
class at Grant High School. California was the goal of many. John	116 _____
Steinbeck had not yet, in 1934, revised our thinking.	125 _____
And now I was one of the lucky ones going to this glorious	138 _____
place where people made movies all day and danced the night	149 _____
away. I was escaping the clatter of typewriters in business school	160 _____
and going instead to college. As I stood there in the smoky light	173 _____
in my neat navy blue dress, which Mother had measured a	184 _____
fashionable twelve inches from the floor when I made it, and with	196 _____
a five-dollar bill given to me by my father for emergencies rolled	208 _____
in my stocking, I tried to hide my elation from my parents.	220 _____

Needs Work   1 2 3 4 5   Excellent
Paid attention to punctuation

Needs Work   1 2 3 4 5   Excellent
Sounded good

Total Words Read _____

Total Errors − _____

Correct WPM _____

Progress Graph

1. For the first reading of the selection, put a red dot on the line above the selection number to show your correct words-per-minute rate.

2. For the second reading, put a blue dot on the line above the selection number to show your correct words-per-minute rate.

3. Make a graph to show your progress. Connect the red dots from selection to selection with red lines. Connect the blue dots with blue lines.

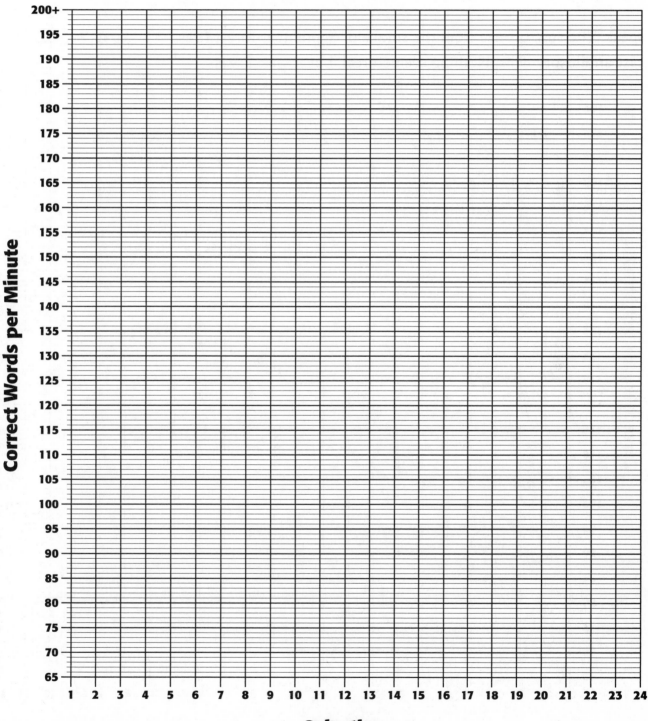

Correct Words per Minute

200+ 195 190 185 180 175 170 165 160 155 150 145 140 135 130 125 120 115 110 105 100 95 90 85 80 75 70 65

1 2 3 4 5 6 7 8 9 10 11 12 13 14 15 16 17 18 19 20 21 22 23 24

Selection

Progress Graph

1. For the first reading of the selection, put a red dot on the line above the selection number to show your correct words-per-minute rate.

2. For the second reading, put a blue dot on the line above the selection number to show your correct words-per-minute rate.

3. Make a graph to show your progress. Connect the red dots from selection to selection with red lines. Connect the blue dots with blue lines.

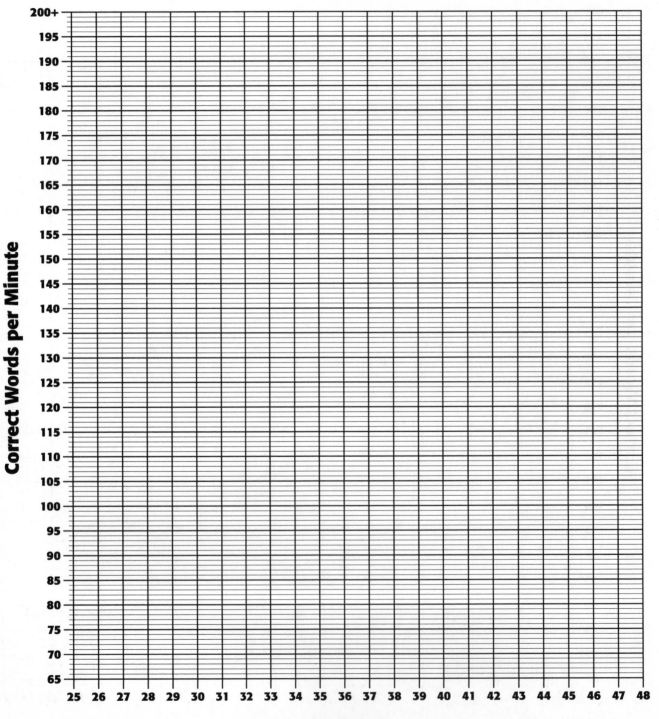

Correct Words per Minute

Selection

Progress Graph

1. For the first reading of the selection, put a red dot on the line above the selection number to show your correct words-per-minute rate.

2. For the second reading, put a blue dot on the line above the selection number to show your correct words-per-minute rate.

3. Make a graph to show your progress. Connect the red dots from selection to selection with red lines. Connect the blue dots with blue lines.

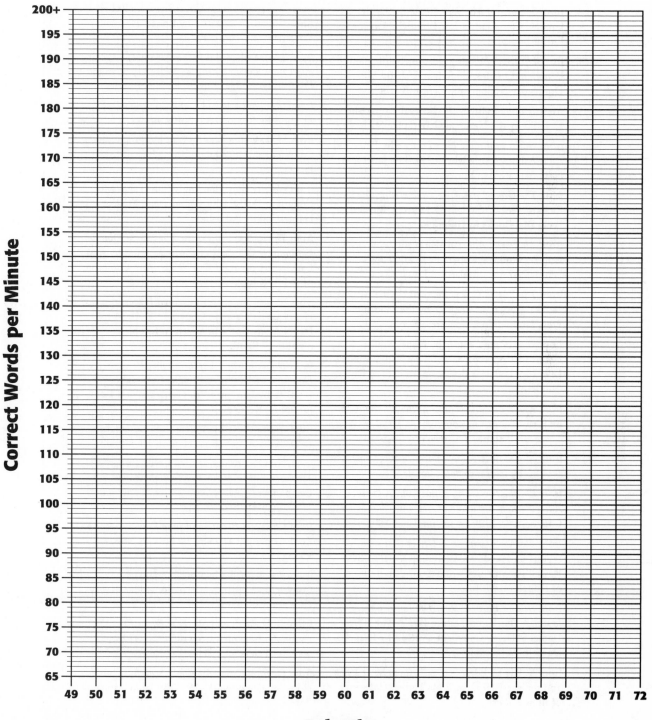

Correct Words per Minute

Selection

Acknowledgments

〰

Grateful acknowledgment is given to the authors and publishers listed below for brief passages excerpted from these longer works.

from *Woman in the Mists: The Story of Dian Fossey and the Mountain Gorillas of Africa* by Farley Mowat. Copyright © 1987 by Farley Mowat Limited. Warner Books.

from *Summer of My German Soldier* by Bette Greene. Copyright © 1973 by Bette Greene. Puffin Books.

from *Lift Every Voice* by Dorothy Sterling and Benjamin Quarles. Copyright © 1965 by Doubleday & Company. Zenith Books.

from *Trial by Ice* by K. M. Kostyal. Copyright © 1999 by the National Geographic Society.

from *Norby and the Oldest Dragon* by Janet and Isaac Asimov. Copyright © 1990 by Janet and Isaac Asimov. Ace Books.

from *The Great Interactive Dream Machine* by Richard Peck. Copyright © 1996 by Richard Peck. Dial Books for Young Readers.

from *An Ocean Apart, a World Away* by Lensey Namioka. Copyright © 2002 by Lensey Namioka. Delacorte Press.

from *The Buried City of Pompeii* by Shelley Tanaka. Copyright © 1997 by the Madison Press Limited. Madison Press Books.

from *Turn of the Century* by Nancy Smiler Levinson. Copyright © 1994 by Nancy Smiler Levinson. Lodestar Books, an affiliate of Dutton Children's Books.

from *Keepers and Creatures at the National Zoo* by Peggy Thomson. Copyright © 1988 by Peggy Thomson. Thomas Y. Crowell.

from *Mountain Light* by Laurence Yep. Copyright ©1985 by Laurence Yep. Harper & Row.

from *On the Bus with Joanna Cole: A Creative Autobiography* by Joanna Cole, with Wendy Saul. Copyright © 1996 by Joanna Cole. Heinemann.

from *Eleanor Roosevelt: A Life of Discovery* by Russell Freedman. Copyright © 1993 by Russell Freedman. Clarion Books, an imprint of Houghton Mifflin.

from *Behind Barbed Wire: The Imprisonment of Japanese Americans During World War II* by Daniel S. Davis. Copyright © 1982 by Daniel S. Davis. E. P. Dutton.

from *So Big* by Edna Ferber. Copyright © 1924 and renewed 1952 by Edna Ferber. University of Illinois Press.

from *A Long Hard Journey: The Story of the Pullman Porter* by Patricia and Fredrick McKissack. Copyright © 1989 by Patricia and Frederick McKissack. Walker & Company.

from *Sally Ride: America's First Woman in Space* by Carolyn Blacknall. Copyright ©1984 by Carolyn Blacknall. Dillon Press.

from "Appetizer" from *Ghost Traps* by Robert H. Abel. Copyright © 1991 by Robert H. Abel. University of Georgia Press.

from "My Mother and Father" from *The Leaving and Other Stories* by Budge Wilson. Copyright © 1990 by Budge Wilson. Philomel Books.

from *Matilda* by Roald Dahl. Copyright © 1988 by Roald Dahl. Puffin Books.

from *Snake's Daughter* by Gail Hosking Gilberg. Copyright © 1997 by the University of Iowa Press.

from *Now Is Your Time!* by Walter Dean Myers. Copyright © 1991 by Walter Dean Myers. HarperCollins Publishers.

from *The Kidnapped Prince: The Life of Olaudah Equiano* by Olaudah Equiano, adapted by Ann Cameron. Copyright © 1995 by Ann Cameron. Alfred A. Knopf.

from "Prime Time" from *Colored People* by Henry Louis Gates Jr. Copyright © 1994 by Henry Louis Gates Jr. Alfred A. Knopf, a division of Random House.

from *Dolphin Man: Exploring the World of Dolphins* by Laurence Pringle. Copyright © 1995 by Laurence Pringle. Atheneum Books for Young Readers.

from *Marie Curie* by Angela Bull. Copyright © 1986 by Angela Bull. Hamish Hamilton.

from "An Occurrence at Owl Creek Bridge" by Ambrose Bierce, from *The Twilight Zone Companion* by Marc Scott Zicree. Copyright © 1982 by Marc Scott Zicree.

from *Charlotte Brontë and Jane Eyre* by Stewart Ross. Copyright © 1997 by Stewart Ross. Viking.

from *Robots Rising* by Carol Sonenklar. Copyright © 1999 by Carol Sonenklar. Henry Holt and Company.

from *Only Earth and Sky Last Forever* by Nathaniel Benchley. Copyright © 1972 by Nathaniel Benchley. Harper & Row.

from *Drifting Snow: An Arctic Search* by James Houston. Copyright © 1992 by James Houston. Puffin Books.